Digital Branding Fever

Digital Branding Fever

Dr. Athanasios Poulis
Dr. Ioannis Rizomyliotis
Dr. Kleopatra Konstantoulaki

BEP BUSINESS EXPERT PRESS

First published in 2017 by
Business Expert Press, LLC
222 East 46th Street, New York, NY 10017
www.businessexpertpress.com

ISBN-13: 978-1-94709-882-4 (paperback)
ISBN-13: 978-1-94709-883-1 (e-book)

Business Expert Press Digital and Social Media Marketing and Advertising Collection

Collection ISSN: 2333-8822 (print)
Collection ISSN: 2333-8830 (electronic)

Cover and interior design by S4Carlisle Publishing Services Private Ltd., Chennai, India

First edition: 2017

10 9 8 7 6 5 4 3 2 1

Printed in the United States of America.

Abstract

Your first step as a business is the most important one. When crafting a digital branding strategy, you want longevity and that is why you must appeal to your consumer demographics. That's the only way to succeed! It is extremely important to understand the meaning and the value of the brand for each target audience in order to develop an effective digital marketing mix. Of course, the value of the brand for a web-based company may have heightened importance because of the intangible nature of the web. Bottom line is that you always need to keep it simple and give a WOW experience!

The game is changing and you need to step up! Digital branding is the creation and development of communications strategies, specifically for brands to have a meaningful context on the web. Branding is not what you say but what you do! As we learn more about branding and its tie to growing a known product, the answer to whether we should brand is simple. If we want to create a niche and dominate it, we need to shape that niche, to define it, and to use several different approaches. In this book, we will analyze those approaches and create together step by step your digital branding strategy and give your consumers an unforgettable experience.

Keywords

brand experience, digital branding, digital strategies, social media branding

Contents

CHAPTER 1

The Digital Fever

In this chapter, you will read:

1. It's all digital
2. Who is watching you?
3. Basic rules of digital brand engagement
4. Can digital brand engagement replace advertising?
5. Popular brand-engagement misconceptions
6. Effective digital brand engagement

Introduction

The ideas associated with the way businesses used to market a service, brand, or product, are today somehow not sufficient. Consumers enjoy buying, but do not enjoy being "sold to," which now means the overall approach requires changes. The act of reaching consumers now involves engaging with them as well as being able to show these consumers that a company really cares about matching up with their requirements with what it has to offer.

For many marketers, one of their largest learning curves is associated with understanding the actual value and concept of a specific brand along with the importance associated with brand building in regard to digital marketing. Today, the industry in which businesses operate moves at a lightning speed with technologies that are constantly evolving, viral videos, algorithm updates, the emergence of social-media platforms, streams associated with memes, the increase in mobile adoption, and so much more. With all these going on, it becomes easy for many businesses to forget that one thing that remains a constant through all these changes and this has to do with the brand. As companies continue to push new boundaries in association to marketing activities with this fast-paced digital environment, it is important to still maintain fundamentals in association with brand building based on long-term success.

The digital landscape continues to grow in the form of an active and living environment whereby consumers can be reached instantly, but the way this will be achieved also needs to evolve. In some cases, ideas of disrupting a person in order to display what a company is about can have undesirable effects, which can drive these consumers away from digital landscapes altogether. An example of this would be when video advertisements based on something that is totally unrelated interrupts what the person is watching on a medium such as YouTube in the middle of the video. It is far better for businesses to gain an understanding of where and who their audience is and then proceed in creating approaches that are more organic in order to reach them, which won't take the viewer out of an experience, but rather add to it.

The principles associated with digital brand engagement explain the approaches that augment or replace the traditional type of "one-way" advertising messages that are aimed at an audience with the strategies that are able to build up a connection in the way of two-way conversations with audiences. These conversations should be aimed at truly engaging with consumers as well as assist them in building up relationships with that brand. The CMOs (Chief Marketing Officers) will continue to require more sophisticated approaches in order to maintain the attentions of audiences, which have become ever more demanding. Digital brand engagement involves disciplined principles that when they are applied in the correct manner are able to reinvent, grow, and connect brands with audiences in an intimate way.

Basically put, digital brand engagement is based on redefining marketing in association with the "modern" digital era, in the way of creating meaningful connections with audiences in the way of leveraging the online tools and ecosystems. Tom Gallego from forbes.com states that the use of apps monitoring social buzz as well as the creation and launching of influence-based marketing campaigns, can form an important part of brand-engagement strategies. The brand of a company has a service or product that can assist consumers; how they are able to communicate this with their audiences is what will result in the defining difference.

It's All Digital

The traditional-based marketing is associated with a one-to-many approach. This means that the business is able to reach larger audiences; however, the message will be solely between a brand and a person who views this advertising. In the social world, marketing is often labeled as a one-to-many approach and is able to achieve that the initial responders of this marketing can now have relationships with a brand as well as the marketplace. This opens possibilities related to far richer experiences, involving consumption between the digital networks that allows for a mass participation that stretches across hours or day opposed to a few minutes. These types of experiences are reliant on engagement which provides a way for the brands to collect real-time and accurate information that are associated with reactions of these fans.

Branding is the type of tool used to develop as well as maintain competitive advantages. In the somewhat noisy digital media world, staying competitive is even more challenging. There is a big difference between a brand and the brand name. Brand names are tangible and consumers can view them. The actual brand exists only in the minds of consumers in regard to what they will be thinking when hearing this name. The building of strong brands in this age of digital is crucial. Even though branding was always of importance, when considering the current online environment and the constant changing behaviors of users, here are some of the obvious benefits associated with branding:

- The online users have become more and more autonomous. With instant information on demand, the users have become spoiled for choice in regard to services and products. Brands that are well defined are vital for a business to distinguish their services or products from their competitors.
- Brands now have a decreased control when it comes to what consumers are saying about their business online. This is because the users now have complete access to what other users have to say, which makes heavy influences on their decisions on a purchase.
- Online customer relationships today rarely end after a sale. This means that brand building within this digital environment must

take advantage of this in order to convert those "one-time customers" into a coveted brand loyalist.

- The funnel model is obsolete, and today there are a number of touch points whereby users will engage with different brands. However, branding guarantees the consolidated message.

- Over and above owned and paid media, strong digital branding will have advantages over earned media such as brand advocates and communities.

- It is important to know that branding will not only be about a service or product, it is also about customer services, sales process, social engagement, the companies' employees, and everything else in between.

- Branding was always based on connectedness, and digital is able to heighten this connectedness of people, brands and things.

Most marketers are aware that integrated marketing is one of the factors related to success within digital environments. Strong brands will support all these channels indirectly and directly so that both resources and time will need to be set aside for brand building through the process of digital marketing. Because of the fact that branding is based on the development of emotional connections, strong brands always have influencers, advocates, followers, and fans who will actively promote these brands. To achieve the most from integrated digital marketing, it is important that businesses do not overlook how important brand building really is. Companies should define their brands and what they stand for, give thought to what drives this brand, and focus on how consumers perceive these brands in each aspect of a business.

Who Is Watching You?

Any relevant brand understands the importance of the customer in the decision-making process. If that golden rule isn't followed, there is always the risk of getting low-quality leads that might not guarantee 100 percent loyalty. It's important to understand that customers go through various stages with the brand. They might not be ready to purchase anything the first time round. The most important thing is providing relevant content for the consumers at every purchasing stage. Thereafter, leveraging the content properly moving the customers from one stage to the next should be the logical next move. Understanding the customer life cycle and meeting the needs of the customers, the brand should enjoy increased conversions as well as engagement. It's also a good way to develop brand loyalty to allow viral sharing of the relevant information to potential customers.

The first step to successful online branding involves the business owner understanding what the business stands for and the goals that should be accomplished. The business owner needs to understand how the consumers perceive the business as well as both the short and long-term objectives. With these objectives, it's easy to find a good foundation to build the brand identity of any business. It's ideal for any business to have a branding team in place to handle the entire project. Such a team should have the objectives and standards in existence. If they are not available, they can always be developed to meet the company's branding needs. To achieve these strategies, there are some branding assets that should already be in place. Basically, it is a branding checklist that contains assets such as internal messages, core messages, targeted messages, the look and feel, and also the identity of the business. With these assets, it's easy for the business owner to understand what the business needs to reveal to the consumers.

Over the years, consumers have become incredibly complex, especially with various advancements in technology and the Internet. Consumers expect a certain level of treatment as well as relevant but controlled experiences. A business owner needs to find a way to meet the consumer's expectations by delivering the right offers through the right channels and in the right time frame. The first thought would be to find the existing consumer information and throw everything at it until something comes up. Of course, such data is necessary and excellent in the right situation; it might not exactly address the problem the audience might be facing. Consumers will definitely tune out if they are not getting what they want from any business. Every business needs to know what the target audience needs to hear. If possible, creating profiles that identify the needs of the consumers can allow the business to find customized strategies that satisfy these needs. Such profiles can be used over various platforms to achieve the best results with regard to digital branding.

Because the business has already identified the audience as well as the demographics, the next step is finding out the problems the audience might be facing. Next, the business needs to identify the products or services that solve the audience problems. Such solutions can be achieved by using various tools. For instance, the business needs to find out the specific keywords used by audience when searching for specific products. With the right keywords, the business can optimize content on its sites, allowing consumers to find the best content to satisfy their problems. With such a direct approach, it's easy for any business to cater to the needs of the audience and satisfy them without fail.

Once the business owner understands the business brand and also identifies the problems the audience might be facing, the next step is determining the middle ground. In simple words, the business owner needs to find the intersection that determines what he or she wants to reveal about the business and what the audience need to hear. Here, it's mostly a discovery phase that should be based on information. One good thing about this stage is the fact that there is no need for costly focus groups or surveys to help the business owner identify the middle ground. Currently, there are numerous of social-media tools and search techniques that can provide the relevant consumer behavioral information for the best results.

If a proper analysis of the data is conducted, it's easy to find out a few important things about the business such as the following:

- Are the marketing and business goals currently in use by the business still relevant?
- Compared to the competition, is the brand still relevant?
- Are there any available positioning opportunities in the current marketplace?
- What's the best way to prioritize services and products to serve the audience better?
- Are there any gaps in the search engine optimization (SEO) techniques that are not being utilized?

Basic Rules of Digital Brand Engagement

Can Digital Brand Engagement Be an Alternative to Advertising?

The word "brand" is a unique identity that is given to a product line or product, and "branding" is the process of creation for this unique identity that creates impressions in the mind of the consumers. It is very important to create brands because of the fact that every day more and even more products are emerging onto the markets, and companies have to do something that is distinctive in order to stand out opposed to getting lost with the others. Good brands are the ones that are able to achieve distinguished impressions on consumers. In the age of digital, newer tools have been created for the promotions of brands. Digital brand engagement is one of those effective "new-age" tools for the development of successful brands. This has to do with a presence of a brand on digital media and its participation in an active way on the different online platforms. This tool assists in making consumers aware of a brand as well as a way to communicate with consumers.

Once a brand has being created, the following step involves promoting it as well as making consumers aware that it exists. Advertising happens to be one of these ways but also comes with its own set of demerits. The marketers of today need to have an understanding that they can no longer impose messages on consumers. Communication has drastically evolved over the years and today communication that is regarded as effective is the type whereby both parties are able to actively participate. For this reason "branding" requires conversation. Older business models that involved pushing product and messages are outdated, and driving the brand impression is just not enough. The establishment of connection and providing an experience is actually what attaches consumers to brands, which is possible through the process of brand engagement.

What is known as the "digital revolution" has transformed everything as we know it in the 21st century. This means that marketing scenarios have changed drastically from previous years. Consumers are a lot more informed today and this is all to do with the Internet. In addition, everyone today will have their own online presence whether it be Instagram, Twitter, Facebook, other social platforms or a combination of all. So, this is by far one of the best mediums for companies to engage with customers. Interaction is easily possible in just about every method possible online, therefore, making digital brand engagement ideal.

Digital brand engagement is a very effective technique used to initiate connections with various prospects. It also offers all the advantages of two-way communication. In addition, it is able to account for personalization with a brand. Advertising on the other hand is merely a technique used to create awareness of a service or product existence. It is a type of one-way communication whereby marketers are only able to convey a message to prospects, but the end users are unable to talk back. Some of the stronger aspects of digital brand engagement over advertising include some of the following:

- *Attracting Attention:* Companies can continue to shout messages at potential customers and will never receive a response. In contrast, when a company is able to have active conversations with consumers, they are able to achieve what they really are looking for and this is their attention.
- *Inspiration Compared to Interruption:* Consumers are in search of brands that will inspire them. Advertising is mainly viewed as a type of interruption, which is usually the type of advertisements that appear during commercial breaks when watching television shows or advertisement videos that appear before just about all the YouTube views. Therefore, engagement is often a mode based on inspiration compared to that of interruption.
- *The Investment Factor:* It is well known that the mass-media advertising campaigns are associated with excessive costs. Even though digital advertising is a more affordable option, it can also result in wastage of time and resources. On the other hand, brand engagement is one of the more favorable options as it linked to comparatively lower costs.
- *Building of Relationships:* Brand engagement allows for brands to build up a relationship with their customers. It is able to create an emotional attachment with consumers for a brand. Advertising really lacks interaction, which means it is not a method that can be utilized to build up relationships with consumers.

- *Enhancing Brand Reputation and Gaining Trust:* The release of an advertisement will not be a guarantee that customers will be receiving the best services or products, but being able to provide experiences.
- *Feedback:* Brands can obtain suggestions on how to improve through platforms such as social media. Customers can now share in on their reasons as to why they are unhappy or dissatisfied with a brand. In turn, the brand can then work on a way to remedy or remove these grievances. Engagement is also an effective method to retain customers once they have been attained.

When considering the aspects that have been listed previously, digital brand engagement is recognized as a real winner, but advertising still holds its place within the organizations in the process of creating awareness. Ultimately, both these mediums should be utilized in collaboration to each other and the core focus of a business should be based on association with consumers. Digital advertising is useful in creating awareness on the different social-media platforms. Once consumers are provided with this knowledge, brands can now begin to exchange dialogues with these consumers. For this reason, digital brand engagement is known as an efficacious tool that is beneficial to new-age marketers in order to offer their customers as well as prospects a far better type of brand experience, which translates into the creation of a brand that is successful.

Popular Misconceptions Associated with Brand Engagement That Can Derail Digital Campaigns

A logo for a company is not its brand, and those attention-grabbing tactics can actually result in turning consumers away. Branding is recognized as a tricky and complex practice and happens to be all-encompassing and multidisciplinary. This is why there are so many individuals who have misinterpreted what brand engagement is really all about. The majority of the digital-marketing campaigns can run amok when they do not integrate correctly with their efforts associated with branding. Following are seven important misconceptions that cause issues for the digital marketers in search of a way to engage with consumers in regard to their specific brand strategies.

A Logo Is Sufficient

Big brands have become synonymous when it comes to their splashy and big logos and since then, most of the laypeople are unable to differentiate brands from what happens to be just packaging. In order to engage with the consumers, branding has to be executed in the form of a full discipline. Value proposition, messaging, organizational ethos, persona, and differentiation are some of the important elements that a company's branding should be able to cohesively quantify. It is only when the consumers are able to clearly identify these particular aspects of brands will they open up to engagement.

Social Media Is the Best Method to Increase Engagement

Certain individuals misunderstand that engagement means a direct type of consumer-to-organization communication. However, this is just one of the components that results in true engagement. The focus of this narrow definition can result in a failure in a digital-marketing campaign. Social media happens to be just one of these channels for connection. Studies have gone onto prove that the best methods to engage will involve multichannel efforts.

Go for Emotional, Evocative, and Loud

It has become an increasingly difficult task to break through noise present on the global marketplace of today. The competition among the brands is no longer just relegated to zip codes. This often leads to a conclusion that is very poor that the best way for a brand to engage is to be bold and splashy. In more cases than not, the successful digital-marketing campaigns happen to be an antithesis of these ideas. They are actually reliant on a carefully measured budget and sound metrics. They also place the needs of the consumers above their own needs. Being loud and splashy can risk these objectives in the way of making them appear that it is just about a brand's needs to gain attention.

No Sales Is Equal to No Engagement

Sales happen to be one of the important brand-engagement metrics. However, there are also other types of engagement factors that will contribute to the organization's understanding in association to its positioning.

A few of these factors cannot be quantified readily. An example, powerful and extraordinary word of mouth will increase page hits, which are a marker of fantastic engagement.

Only the Costly and Extravagant Ads Will Drive Engagement

In many cases, some of the largest brand-engagement campaigns will appear in *Adweek*. These are the types of brands that hired expensive and fancy agencies, and these agencies achieved phenomenal digital shares. Engagement should and can be the key factor on any aspect of a digital-marketing campaign. Social-media activities and valuable content can work together to entitle healthy engagement. This is also possible through stimulating customer-to-customer activity, offering solutions to issues, and hosting chats. Businesses need to develop the processes that will guarantee outstanding customer service as well as invite the users to share the success of a brand. Companies also have to be honest and realistic about the failures of a brand.

A Focus on Content Marketing Is the Ideal Way to Increase Engagement

This is very similar to the misconceptions surrounding social media. Content marketing is unable to solve all problems. In some cases, one of the better ways to engage with the consumers is to simply say "hello." Content is a fantastic way to deliver value, but at the same time a circuitous method to engage. It is also better for businesses to diverse their efforts and not to solely rely on content to tell the story of their brand.

Brand Engagement Is Separate from the Rest of the Digital-Marketing Campaign

At its very heart, this happens to be the central theme for all the previous misconceptions. Brand engagement must involve every person within an organization, which should include the operations-team members. The reason for this is that engagement actually means that a brand willing extends its reach to the consumers. True brand-engagement is always an open-door policy. Whether these doors are opened to the brand's products, material, ideas, or people, they seek an interaction between not only the consumers but also with their most "valuable" assets.

Effective Digital Brand Engagement

Successful digital branding or the use of digital networks to convey and build a company's position can become the deciding factors associated with decline or growth. Nowadays, it is required to have a specific approach of marketing: in the form of a digital brand experience. Consumers connect to the different social-media channels at all times of the day or night, 365 days in the year. But what does this mean in regard to digital marketing? People no longer want to be barraged with massive amounts of information; they prefer to rather engage with materials by their own choice. Businesses are now unable to push their brands, but rather need to inspire an interaction through the process of conversing and listening instead.

Nurturing relationships through communication is regarded as the quickest methods to engage with customers. However, the management of digital engagement and digital branding strategies is the sole way to build a business. It is very important for businesses to know the differences between earned, owned, and paid media and to then tailor their strategies to a current marketplace using these three important types of marketing.

Earned Media refers to "free" promotions that are generated through word of mouth and social media. By knowing what type of technologies are available, it is easier to optimize and manage your strategies.

Paid Media refers to anything that has been paid for, which increases the visibility of the brand. An example of this would be Facebook advertising that allows companies to target an audience based on locations, demographics, and a variety of other metric types. Other examples will include pay per click (PPC) and search engine marketing (SEM). Ad blocking will continue to increase; counteracting this will be the engagement ads. These work in the method of expanding a "lightbox" into a bigger window when a user hovers over this box for more than two seconds. The larger box will then display videos, purchasing along with other types of brand interactions in order to attract the attention of customers.

Owned Media is any type of channel that a company has full control over, which includes online profiles and websites. The foundation to using websites fully is based on keeping it up to date, relevant, and continuously providing high-quality and new content. The content should never remain static on websites, but rather be distributed through other channels. One of the best methods to raise good content is the use of infographics. Combined with video, popularity associated with infographics is in fact growing. Currently, this visual data type is shared more frequently by the Twitter users compared to any other type of content. One of the advantages of infographics is the method in which it is able to clearly lay out research and statistics. The audiences respond well when information is interesting and relevant, as well as conceptually or factually derived from customer comments and social media. It is also able to provide researchers with potential blog topics that are new. These charts can easily be divided or broken down into more-in-depth and smaller posts and articles that can be distributed to a target audience and then utilized on the company's website.

On the other hand, real time does translate to real profits. The inclusion of live broadcasts, virtual reality (VR) clips and video segments is guaranteed to attract bigger audiences. The companies that make use of real-time posts that provide relevant coverage in regard to affairs and events, which appeal to fans and consumers, is able to grow audiences in a more effective way compared to those that only focus on the product-centric narratives.

The banner advertisements were and still are a widely used method associated with direct-response campaigns in order to urge consumers to take advantage of time-restricted deals. But when it comes to digital marketing and, more specifically, the display advertising can be far more than only generating those immediate clicks. Marketers are now offered opportunities in developing campaigns with the purposes of branding. The digital-branding-based campaigns have become increasingly effective in the abilities to understand and track the browsing behavior of user. Marketers are now able to focus their efforts on the building of brand awareness and brand recall (as a long term goal) rather than focusing on short-term conversions. Data associated with past-purchase information, search history, and demographics can be utilized to create branding campaigns that are extremely effective.

Brands take a lot of hard work. However, those successful brands are the types that work smarter. Here are some tips on how to achieve digital branding success.

- *Push versus Pull Marketing:* When social media first began, many of the experts were convinced about the "push verses pull" marketing strategies. However, today consumers refused to be "force-fed" but have chosen to rather be led to tables if they have made the decision to "eat." This resulted in tables packed with irresistible treats for consumers to enjoy. This is when a brand is able to turn from sinking into swimming. Today, consumers only want the service, products, and content from the companies or brands that they trust, like, and know. However, the building of these relationships takes some time and it is definitely not sufficient to just join these conversations in the way of flooding these gates. Currently, success can be found when a company is able to stand out in the form of an "authority leader" as well as a connected brand.
- *Brand Restrictions within Digital Marketing:* The more that the brands try to push, the faster the targeted markets set up boundaries. Humans suffer from what is known as "information overload" and the continuous reminders, offers, articles, messages, and so on, have the targeted markets feeling confused and overwhelmed. This has resulted in consumers who have built-in filters that funnel out junk and they only keep what fulfills a professional or personal need. When a company is unable to provide solutions or the content is unable to answer the "why" behind services or products, the target market usually will not give this business any of its attention.
- *Maintaining Consistency in Online Activities:* The goal of any business online is to standout to achieve results. To achieve this goal, companies need to grow their authority and brand organically. Communication needs to be concise and engagement needs to be continuous: This includes SEO strategies, editorial calendars, and the best practices for "social-media" digital marketing. This is done in the way of conveying content in such a way that it can assist the target market in solving issues as well as a way to engage the target audience in a solution. Engagement is important with the

online communities that provide a way for consumers to feel safer in regard to what they can expect from a brand or business. Today companies should rather focus on developing their brands over a period of time and avoid rushing in and bombarding consumers with a brand. The successful brands engage with purpose that will be driven naturally.

Summary

Engagement happens to be the word commonly used by the different brands that describe actions taken on the social-media platforms. However, this particular term has been overused and taken for granted in the way that just about any of the social-media posts is able to engage with audiences. In reality, regardless of the amount of followers that can be viewed on a post or even interact with this post, only the people who take a further action are the ones who are really engaging with a brand or business. Fans happen to be central to any of the brands in the way of driving forces to achieve long-term growth. But how do brands clearly define the way in which they should progress in engaging with these fans and what is the purpose behind this engagement?

The definition of true engagement is when consumers deeply connect with a brand, category, or topic and form part of a type of topical microcommunity. These types of "connected activity" are divided into four subcategories:

- Contribution, this is when audiences create their very own content, which is commonly referred to as user generated content (UGC)
- Influence, where an audience is influential over the other consumers
- Collaboration, where an audience participated in the content creation with the actual brand or other consumers
- Advocacy, where audiences adopt the sense of affinity and ownership

It is with the engagement strategies that companies are able to advance practices in association to marketing, which is awareness based on a place that the fans actually grow with brands and form a real part of activities opposed to just recipients. Business objectives that can be enforced through these processes are able to drive a variety of actionable outcomes that include purchases, downloads, transactions, signups, and more along with a long-term goal of achieving a retained and loyal user base. It is important to know that engagement will not be achieved from singular posts. The single-post "interactions" are misunderstood as a type of true engagement. However, actual true engagement is achieved through a process of a far longer journey.

Bibliography

Bowden, J. L. H. (2009). The process of customer engagement: A conceptual framework. *Journal of Marketing Theory and Practice, 17*(1), 63-74.

Brodie, R. J., Ilic, A., Juric, B., & Hollebeek, L. (2013). Consumer engagement in a virtual brand community: An exploratory analysis. *Journal of Business Research, 66*(1), 105-114.

Gummerus, J., Liljander, V., Weman, E., & Pihlström, M. (2012). Customer engagement in a Facebook brand community. *Management Research Review, 35*(9), 857-877.

Hollebeek, L. D. (2011). Demystifying customer brand engagement: Exploring the loyalty nexus. *Journal of marketing management, 27*(7-8), 785-807.

Kabadayi, S., & Price, K. (2014). Consumer–brand engagement on Facebook: liking and commenting behaviors. *Journal of Research in Interactive Marketing, 8*(3), 203-223.

Malthouse, E. C., Calder, B. J., & Vandenbosch, M. (2016). Creating brand engagement on digital, social and mobile media (pp. 85-101). In R. J. Brodie, L. D. Hollebeek, & J. Conduit (Eds.). *Customer Engagement*. New York: Routledge.

Martí, J., Bigné, E., & Hyder, A. (2014). Brand engagement. In L. Moutinho, E. Bigné, & A. K. Manrai (Eds.). *The Routledge Companion to the Future of Marketing* (pp. 250-257). London: Routledge.

Tiago, M. T. P. M. B., & Veríssimo, J. M. C. (2014). Digital marketing and social media: Why bother? *Business Horizons, 57*(6), 703-708.

Uzunoğlu, E., & Kip, S. M. (2014). Brand communication through digital influencers: Leveraging blogger engagement. *International Journal of Information Management, 34*(5), 592-602.

Vadivu, V. M., & Neelamalar, M. (2015, May). Digital brand management: A study on the factors affecting customers' engagement in Facebook pages. In *Smart Technologies and Management for Computing, Communication, Controls, Energy and Materials (ICSTM), 2015 International Conference on* (pp. 71-75). Chennai: IEEE.

Van Doorn, J., Lemon, K. N., Mittal, V., Nass, S., Pick, D., Pirner, P., & Verhoef, P. C. (2010). Customer engagement behavior: Theoretical foundations and research directions. *Journal of Service Research, 13*(3), 253-266.

Vivek, S. D., Beatty, S. E., & Morgan, R. M. (2012). Customer engagement: Exploring customer relationships beyond purchase. *Journal of Marketing Theory and Practice, 20*(2), 122-146.

CHAPTER 2

Keep It Simple and Give a WOW Experience

In this chapter, you will read:

1. Who are we talking to?
2. Are the customers finding you?
3. The users' journey
4. Keep it simple and give a WOW experience
5. Turn increased value in cold hard cash

Introduction

To guarantee future sales, numerous businesses rely on consistent branding over time. However, such results have been somersaulted by social media and search engines. Therefore, brands that understand the need for visibility, going viral, and finding potential customers, always win over their competitors. Currently, brand relevance has become more recognizable than differentiation with the competitors. Brand relevance refers to the proper alignment of the identity and strategy to illuminate a benefit, which addresses the needs, wants, or desires of any consumer. Thanks to brand relevance there is an increased focus on the needs of the consumer thereby enhancing the consumer's experience. As a result, the consumer can count on a consistent experience from any media outlet online or otherwise.

Well, the need for branding for any business can't be underestimated. Digital branding has become more prevalent in the last few years with more consumers turning online for their shopping preferences. If a business is properly branded, consumers can find it effortlessly online. On the other hand, consumers can recommend the business to their friends and numerous other connections thereby improving the brand's identity.

As already explained, unlike traditional marketing, digital branding combines various techniques, such as digital marketing and Internet branding, to develop a strong brand identity over various online venues. Whether social media or third-party listing sites, a properly branded business has more visibility online. Basically, if a customer performs an online search of the business, the results will prove to be authoritative, especially if the website is leading in the search engine results.

There are some notable differences between traditional and digital branding. Here are some of the notable ones that every business should know.

Easy Comprehension: Currently, millennials are leading most of the consumer markets. That's partly the reason why online markets have become more prevalent than traditional brick and mortar shops. Everything can be accessed online from any smart device. Therefore, millennials understand everything there is to do online. When it comes to traditional branding methods, it might be tough to teach the millennials the old ways. On the other hand, digital branding is easy, fast, and very comprehensible by everyone. It seems simple enough especially everything has become paperless.

Cost-Effective: Traditional methods include print media (magazine ads, newspaper ads, newsletters, or brochures), direct mail (catalogues, flyers, or post cards), broadcast media (radio and television ads), and also telemarketing. With these traditional branding methods, the business needs to actively go out and find the customers. Previously, these techniques have a high success rate but they are very costly. On the other hand, it's tough to measure the consumer response. Of course, there are numerous companies that rely on traditional branding methods. However, digital branding has become popular for many reasons. For instance, it is less costly. Some of the common digital branding methods commonly in use include search engine optimization, social-media marketing, Google ads, websites, and also banner ads. Here, the customers are already in place waiting for the business to contact them.

In comparison, digital branding is considered less costly than traditional branding for all the reasons named previously. Of course, to achieve the best results, most companies rely on both methods. It's guaranteed that both traditional and digital branding can guarantee a strong brand identity.

The bottom line, though, is to have a robust picture of how the customers behave and act in your market.

Who Are We Talking to?

Audience Targeting: Segmenting a Company's Branding Efforts to an Audience That Falls within the Company's Target Market

When it comes to the direct-response campaigns, objectives associated with audience targeting will often be based on reaching the ideal audience. In the way businesses are targeting these audiences, marketers attempt to achieve immediate sales and website visits. This audience-targeting method is also useful to grow brand recognition. In the way of capturing attention of the brand's target market that have been identified, opposed to just the consumers who may have demonstrated an intention to purchase, the marketers are able to raise brand awareness with a qualified and larger audience. Audience targeting is easy to employ to match up to numerous branding objectives. Digital marketers are able to increase their reach in the way of serving their ads to a new audience or they can reinforce their branding initiatives within a current defined target segment.

This fine-tuned segmentation is possible in the way of leveraging data from the users' browsing history and activity across various sites in order to develop sophisticated and professional user profiles. These profiles are further defined by contextual, demographic, and geographic variables, which empower the brand strategists with the opportunities to apply a budget to definitive audience groups such as "First-time parents from New York," or "Recent, Female College-Grad."

Search Retargeting: Involves Establishing Brand Recall with Users That Already Search for Specific Services or Products

Search retargeting is able to enable a brand to find or reach those users who happen to be already searching for specific services or products. This is achievable in a few different ways. One way is targeting interest-based keywords that emphasize the unique traits of a brand. Because of the fact that these consumers are recognized as in-market users, they often possess an increased level of receptiveness along with an increase with an intent to buy. In addition, brands are able to set parameters in order to serve their ads when the users are searching for their competitors.

Retargeting: Boosting Efforts for the Consumers Who Already Have Preliminary-Brand Awareness to Increase Further Consideration

Today there are several types of retargeting. This includes retargeting people who have previously visited a website, searched for a product or opened up an e-mail. Regardless of how the consumers arrived at their first engagement, the act of retargeting is very powerful in the way that it is able to convert the consumers with limited or little exposure to the brand into consumers with an increased interest in the way of continually delivering impressions that are meaningful and increases further consideration. According to a study by ValueClick Media and comScore, retargeting has been revealed as a type of display-ad strategy that has the "greatest impact" in relation to brand lift. The retargeted display ads resulted in 1,046 percent lift in association to brand-searchers within 30 days after exposure. Retargeting was also able to achieve the biggest lift in association to site visits within this same month of exposure by 726 percent. These figures suggest that retargeting, re-engagement strategies offer great advantages when in search of a way to increase engagement and brand awareness.

Programmatic Premium: Combines the Efficiency and Power of Real-Time Bidding with Brand Security of Premium Inventory

Retargeting, audience retargeting and search retargeting allow a company to engage effectively with all relevant users. This is possible no matter where they happen to be on the web. But many marketers want to know how to make sure their ads are present on the sites that guarantee brand security? Programmatic Premium offers a way to bridge the gaps between super-premium inventory and RTB (Real-Time Bidding) and then automates the various tedious steps, which advertisers were once tasked with.

However, with the definite reduction in regard to "direct" buying of inventory, many marketers are apprehensive of where their advertisements will be displayed. Serving these ads on inappropriate, user-generated, or mature sites can result in disastrous effects to the image of a brand. For this reason, marketers should be choosing to serve their ads on the inventory, which is classified as "premium" and currently available. This "premium" is not overcrowded, well-lit inventory and brand-safe.

Creative Optimization: Tailoring the Creative of a Business to Match Up to Its Branding Objectives

Over and above reaching the correct consumers, branding that is strong needs the correct messaging. For example, the creation of brand recognition and long-lasting recall is not always achieved with the use of the very same creative approach that usually drives those immediate sales. The recipe to the creation of the correct impact when delivering messaging that is relevant is to use a creative that is able to resonate. This is possible by leveraging the various media options that are available as well as conducting A/B testing to arrive at long-term-based brand awareness, which goes further than the immediate click-throughs. With the growth of the display-ad formats, today there are more options available to convey the story of a brand as well as impart meaningful impressions. For example, rich media that is flash-enabled is able to create banner advertisements, which are dynamic that can include anything from a brief animation onto expandability, which allows for interaction with these ad units. These expandable ads can also include games, surveys, and product feeds that drives messaging and memorability.

The use of A/B tests around image, background, and color or the wording associated with the brand's value proposition or the banner ads can assist marketers in avoiding speculation on the type of creative that will prove to be the most effective and rather focus on making data-driven decisions.

Evaluating Impact

In regard to branding campaigns, CTR (Click-Through Rate) along with the other commonly used metrics for direct responses often do not reveal the entire story. In fact, many Internet users will never click-on these advertisements, but this does not mean that they do not work. One of the valuable metrics known as view-through conversion is able to quantify impact related to these display ads as it accounts for that not all the display ads will trigger immediate actions, but can still have an influence on browsing behavior into the future. The goal behind branding campaigns today is not about driving sales but rather to create awareness around specific traits, needs, or a style that the brand meets, which in turn drives long-term customer loyalty.

The tasks associated with measuring that "long-term customer loyalty" and the other types of positive effects associated with branding campaigns are often regarded as more complex compared to the reliable CTR. However, for those marketers who avoid these branding objectives and choose the traditional types of direct-response campaigns often lose out on this opportunity that is increasingly lucrative. Currently, brand studies, branded search, and brand lift are all the reliable methods used to detect how efficient digital branding is, and can assist marketers in deciding on the best ways in which to design their own branding strategies.

Are the Customers Finding You?

With digital branding becoming very popular for online business owners, it's important to identify the best strategies to guarantee the best results. Some of the most successful online branding techniques are summarized.

Unless the business is a renowned brand, the first branding strategy should be online visibility so that customers will eventually find you. The first step of the process is the consumer taking a smart device and starts learning about a service or product he or she is thinking about buying. Anything that the consumers find online about the business is the current brand relevance. The business owner needs to remember that at every stage of the process, consumers will be comparing that specific brand to any digital experience they have previously gone through. Well, because the business owner has enough control about this, then it's good news. Of course, he or she needs to pay some extra attention to more things besides the look and feel of the brand to the audience.

To guarantee high brand loyalty, the search engine optimization strategies in place need to be buttoned up. The same goes for the social-media strategies as well as the website experience. Here are some useful tips that can nudge the **branding experience** ahead at this point.

- *Improving the Search Engine Optimization Strategy:* Before purchasing anything, consumers always start with search engines. At least 90 percent of consumers rely on search engines for any purchases. About 70 percent of those individuals immediately become organic traffic, meaning that they are not paid. Keep in mind that at least 75 percent of search engine users never leave the first-page results on any search engine. With these statistics, every business owner should be trying to get ahead of the prospects. It means that any business brand exists in the search engine algorithms. Therefore, the need to tweak the algorithm to guarantee first-page result should be the first priority of every business owner. The million dollar question is how a simple website will get to the first page. Well, because customers rely heavily on keywords to find anything online, the business owner needs to integrate a keyword strategy into the website to make sure it's probably customized to find out what the customer needs.

- *Transforming a Website into a Content Hub:* If current and potential customers visit a website regularly, it's likely for the business to become a renowned brand. For that to happen, the site needs to be regularly updated with relevant content. Consumers are looking for help on the site, not just products and services, and that's exactly what the site should provide. Transforming a site into a content hub can be quite effortless. The first thing to do involves starting a blog. To guarantee relevant content for the blog, the owner needs to create an editorial plan. Of course, if there was already a blog in place, it's important to keep everything in tune with the customer profiles. That way, customers get the best information from the site about the products being offered.

- *Active Social-Media Presence:* Currently, business owners care a lot about what strangers have to say and not what the brand reveals about itself. Note that most people can purchase anything depending on social-media mentions. Most consumers also trust online reviews much more compared to personal recommendations.

Therefore, a business needs to pay attention to everything being said about it in the social media and join the chat. The business should also engage the followers by sharing the original content for the site's blog. It's also prudent to engage the followers in the right channels because not everyone is on one specific social-media platform.

In all, digital branding is considered the beta version of the whole process because everything is a test. There is no guaranteed certainty because the online world changes frequently and so do the target audience. It's a very common mistake for most business owners to let digital branding strategies to run their course without any necessary adjustments. There is no way of getting the same results every time by repeating a similar campaign. Therefore, the strategies need to be constantly adjusted to meet the needs of the consumers. If any relevant content has been published and received well, the same procedure can be used to curate fresh content. A good measurement strategy should be in place to check whether everything is working as it should. Even better, the strategy can be used to correct anything that's not working and find a new way to achieve the best results. As a matter of fact, there are numerous tools online that can be used to calculate the success rate of any digital branding strategy.

The Users' Journey

Providing excellent customer service through your online channels can also give your digital branding a huge boost, while at the same time this could create a unique experience for the customer. Instead of picking up the phone, consumers now extend their inquiries or complaints through online platforms. If you fail to respond, or if you do not even provide a way for customers to reach you, it reflects poorly on your digital brand. One bad experience of a single customer can cripple your entire business. You do not want to lose customers by not providing them a means to connect with you. To help sort this problem out, here are some customer service tools that make it quick and easy to respond to all inbound messages.

If you need a suite of tools to extend your customer service online, then ZenDesk is the tool you're looking for. The platform streamlines all your communication channels in one location, and so it's simpler and faster to respond to phone calls, chats, and e-mails.

A great thing about ZenDesk is that it not only provides a means for more effective communication with your customers, but also helps you glean insights into different metrics that affect your business. These can then be used to make necessary changes and offer your target audience the level of customer service they deserve. Responding to customer inquiries in the fastest way possible should always be a priority. This can be easily achieved with the help of LiveChat.

This tool allows you to place a "Chat Now" box right on your website. Customers who land on your site and want to ask something can instantly reach out to you or your support team. As you can imagine, chatting with customers in real-time provides a much better experience compared to making them wait for your e-mail response or call back. An instant response to a customer query can lead to a conversion. And when this adds up, expect to gain tons of additional revenue by simply improving your online customer service.

Keep It Simple and Give a WOW Experience

Each and every company leader who is seeking legitimacy will be aware of that the process of dispersing the brand across a variety of digital platforms is a necessity. Each of the digital platforms will have its own set of dedicated audience in regard to users who will prefer a particular method in interaction compared to others. When a company's brand is able to establish a presence over multiple platforms, it is fundamentally meeting up with potential consumers within its neighborhood. When these companies show that they care enough to pay a visit to these neighborhoods, these consumers become more open to supporting these companies' brands. The connection with customers on social-media platforms such as Google Plus, Twitter, LinkedIn, and Facebook is the standard when it comes to social-media marketing but the other types of engaging digital platforms are free for use and can assist in catapulting a company's prominence in regard to the search engine listings. According to research in regard to posting on these four channels, here is a bit of insight:

YouTube

The entrepreneurs who have not taken advantage of the YouTube platform are really doing themselves a great disservice. It is true that the required content may seem a bit more complex in order to create. However, if the company has already created its own content strategy, it is easy to make use of these same concepts and then just add a camera and a person. The content does not need to be a type of million dollar production, it just needs to be relatable. This can include an employee who sits in front of a curtain and discusses industry-related events or news or to share funny or interesting stories about events that have unfolded in the company that week. The point of this technique is based on being visible and present so that the users who enjoy taking in information through a medium such as videos will really appreciate that a company makes the effort to reach them.

BuzzFeed

Recognized in regard to its "signature listicles" that offer humorous snapshots associated with people's lifestyles along with recaps based on news that is relevant on that day, BuzzFeed has become a popular household name. What many companies do not realize is that anyone is able to create his or her own BuzzFeed channels for free. Companies should aim to craft eye-catching "listicles," which let a target audience understand and know what the company is about. These posts may not make the front-page placement on this platform, but supporters and fans won't be aware of the differences when the company shares these posts on the other different social-media platforms. When a company creates its own BuzzFeed posts and channel, certain consumers are often happy to interact with a business through the type of format that they find appealing and trendy.

Playbuzz

Just about all the users on social-media platforms have at some point wasted a bit of their time in answering one of those personality quizzes, answering a question such as "What color is your personality?" These activities often add in a couple of moments of enjoyment and amusement to a person's day. Companies can take advantage and join in on this fun. Any company is able to create its own free Playbuzz channel and then create a quiz that it can share with its followers. Including these quizzes in a company's digital-content strategy can provide another way to inform and amuse consumers across all the different social-media platforms.

Udemy

Udemy happens to be a marketplace dedicated to online learning. Teachers use this site to set up courses that they sell and the students learn, buy, and browse. A company can also take advantage of brand presence on these platforms. Udemy is also free and consumers use this site to browse through the topics in search of any new ways to educate them. Companies can take advantage of promoting the consumers' "intellectual growth" in the way of offering classes that are free through Udemy, which can teach these consumers more about the company's field of interests. Companies that are able to establish themselves on Udemy in the form of an "instructor" set the company up as a type of authority within their field, while at the same time introducing the brand of the company to a brand-new subculture of individuals.

Turn Increased Value in Cold Hard Cash

For the companies that are involved in building brands or brand portfolios, there are common types of branding challenges that they may face in their effort to capitalize their digital presence. These businesses can benefit in the way of appraising how they are able to face each of these challenges:

Treating a Brand as an Asset

Ongoing pressure associated with delivering short-term financial based results combined with fragmentation of the media often tempts organizations into focusing on measurable results and tactics and then neglects the objectives associated with building assets.

Retaining a Compelling Vision

The vision of a brand has to be able to "differentiate" itself, inspire employees, and resonate with consumers or customers. It also has to be worthwhile to implement and work well overtime in dynamic marketplaces. The visions that usually work are typically multidimensional and are able to adapt to various contexts. They will also employ concepts like organizational values, brand personality, as well as typically move beyond their functional benefits.

The Creation of New Subcategories

The sole way to grow with very rare exceptions is to do with developing "must have" innovations, which define the new subcategories as well as build up barriers, which stop the competitors from obtaining relevance. This necessitates transformational or substantial innovation along with new abilities in order to manage perceptions of these subcategories so that they win.

The Generation of Breakthrough Brand Building

Exceptional ideas along with executions that manage to break free from the clutter are important to bring the vision of a brand to life. These particular ideas along with how they are executed should be seen as more vital compared to the actual size of a company's budget. Today "good" is no longer good enough. What this means is that a company should focus on obtaining ideas from additional sources and to ensure that the correct mechanisms are present in order to distinguish brilliance as well as bring these ideas onto the markets quickly.

Achieving Integrated-Marketing Communication

Integrated-marketing communication (IMC) happens to be more difficult and elusive today in association with the different methods a company is forced to choose from. These can include social media, mobile, digital, sponsorships, advertising, and more. These techniques often compete with one another rather than reinforcing as the media options and scene has become so intricate, dynamic, and complex. In addition, country silos and product reflect isolation and competition opposed to communication and cooperation.

Building Digital Strategies

This particular arena is dynamic and complex and requires a different kind of mindset. The truth of the matter is that audiences are the one in control in this area. This means creative initiatives, new capabilities, and a different approach to working with other types of marketing modalities are needed. This also means the adjustment of the focus of digital marketing from offerings as well as the brand to consumer's sweet spots. These include opinions and activities that they are passionate about or interested in. It also means developing programs around these sweet spots whereby the brand is seen as one of the active partners. An example of this is what Pampers did with the Pampers Village or what the company Avon did in regard to their Walk for Breast Cancer.

Building Brands Internally

It becomes very hard or impossible to achieve integrated-marketing communications that are successful or the type of breakthrough marketing without the employees of a business knowing about this vision or caring about the vision. Brand visions that lack higher purpose often find inspirational challenges close to impossible.

The Maintenance of Brand Relevance

Brands today face three "relevance" threats: less customers purchasing what their brand offers, the emergence of reasons not to buy, and a decrease or lack of energy. Locating as well as responding to each of these threats necessitates an in-depth knowledge and experience of the markets as well as a willingness and need to invest and then change.

Creating Brand Portfolio Strategies That Will Yield Clarity and Synergy

Brands require a well-defined role as well as visions that support these roles. A strategic brand should be able to be resourced and identified along with branded energizers and differentiators need to be created as well as managed.

The Leveraging of Brand Assets to Enable Growth

Brand portfolios need to foster growth in the way of providing new offerings, extending this brand into other product classes or extending a brand vertically. The goal should be based on applying a brand into new contexts where this brand will simultaneously enhance itself and add value. Those businesses engaged in leveraging and building their brand should examine every one of these prevalent challenges and make a decision on which of these are the most vital in order to achieve success. This should be followed by evaluating the degree in which this company's brand is in a deficit in regard to meeting up to one or more of these challenges.

Summary

If there are any businesses that have not initiated their digital branding strategies yet, here are some of the reasons why they should get started immediately. Online shopping has completely transformed everything. People are always on their mobile devices looking for the next thing they are going to buy. If any business is looking to breach the online marketplace, digital branding is the way to do it right. Customers are already in place waiting, the business owner just needs to find the right way to tap into it. Digital branding is almost free, especially with most of the techniques such as social media. Therefore, rather than using traditional methods such as print media that can be quite costly, digital is the way to do it. By constantly engaging people on social media, it's easy to create a trend for your business and get the branding needed. Mixing up both digital and traditional branding might create a good blend that might produce extraordinary results. Trying out the cost-effective branding methods might work perfectly for any new online business looking to beat the competitors.

Digital branding is the best way to reveal a new business into the online world. It needs to be done right to achieve the best results. Any branding strategy that has been put in place needs to cater to the customers at all times. The customer is the center of every business objective. The days of a business pushing their products down the throats of all customers are gone. With a digital branding strategy, the business can cater to the customer's needs and at the same time count on high profits.

Bibliography

Blackston, M., & Lebar, E. (2015). Constructing consumer-brand relationships to better market and build businesses. *Strong Brands, Strong Relationships*, 376.

Chun, H. H., Whan, C., Eisingerich, A. B., & MacInnis, D. J. (2015). Strategic benefits of low fit brand extensions: When and why? *Journal of Consumer Psychology, 25*(4), 577-595.

Cocoran, I. (2013). *The Art of Digital Branding*. New York: Skyhorse Publishing, Inc.

Felix, R., Rauschnabel, P. A., & Hinsch, C. (2017). Elements of strategic social media marketing: A holistic framework. *Journal of Business Research, 70*, 118-126.

Han, K. S. (2016). Exploratory study on effect of brand experience and interactivity of digital signage using virtual reality on attitude. *Indian Journal of Science and Technology, 9*(44).

Hanna, S. A., & Rowley, J. (2015). Rethinking strategic place branding in the digital age. In M. Kavaratzis, G. Warnaby, & G. J. Ashworth (Eds.). *Rethinking Place Branding* (pp. 85-100). Cham: Springer International Publishing.

Keller, K. L. (2016). Reflections on customer-based brand equity: Perspectives, progress, and priorities. *AMS review, 6*(1-2), 1-16.

Klapdor, S., Anderl, E. M., von Wangenheim, F., & Schumann, J. H. (2014). Finding the right words: The influence of keyword characteristics on performance of paid search campaigns. *Journal of Interactive Marketing, 28*(4), 285-301.

Kleppinger, C. A., & Cain, J. (2015). Personal digital branding as a professional asset in the digital age. *American Journal of Pharmaceutical Education, 79*(6), 79.

Landa, R. (2016). Building a brand narrative in the digital age. In R. Landa (Ed.). *Advertising by Design: Generating and Designing Creative Ideas Across Media* (pp. 78-89). Hoboken: John Wiley & Sons Inc.

Lipiäinen, H. S. M., & Karjaluoto, H. (2015). Industrial branding in the digital age. *Journal of Business & Industrial Marketing, 30*(6), 733-741.

Mezofi, D., & Nilsson, A. (2016). Personal branding behind the firewall: An analysis of consultants' perceptions about personal digital branding. Master's thesis, Lund University.

Moran, G., & Muzellec, L. (2017). eWOM credibility on social networking sites: A framework. *Journal of Marketing Communications, 23*(2), 149-161.

Moran, G., Muzellec, L., & Nolan, E. (2014). Consumer moments of truth in the digital context. *Journal of Advertising Research, 54*(2), 200-204.

Rohm, A., Hanna, R., & Crittenden, V. (2017). Connecting social media and traditional media: Best & worst practices. In Campbell, C. L. (Ed.). *The Customer is NOT Always Right? Marketing Orientationsin a Dynamic Business World* (pp. 919-919). Cham: Springer.

Royle, J., & Laing, A. (2014). The digital marketing skills gap: Developing a Digital Marketer Model for the communication industries. *International Journal of Information Management, 34*(2), 65-73.

Singh, S., Sao, A., Nagare, T. B., & Dharmarajan, A. (2017). Role of social media marketing in brand building: The new age marketing strategy. *International Journal of Scientific Research, 5*(9).

Swaminathan, V. (2016). Branding in the digital era: new directions for research on customer-based brand equity. *AMS review, 6*(1-2), 33-38.

Swaminathan, V., Page, K., & Gurhan-Canli, Z. (2007). My brand or our brand: Individual-and group-based brand relationships and self-construal effects on brand evaluations. *Journal of Consumer Research, 34*(2), 248-259.

Tiago, M. T. P. M. B., & Veríssimo, J. M. C. (2014). Digital marketing and social media: Why bother? *Business Horizons, 57*(6), 703-708.

Yoon, D., & Youn, S. (2016). Brand experience on the website: Its mediating role between perceived interactivity and relationship quality. *Journal of Interactive Advertising, 16*(1), 1-15.

Youn, S., & Jin, S. V. (2017). Reconnecting with the past in social media: The moderating role of social influence in nostalgia marketing on Pinterest. *Journal of Consumer Behaviour.*

Young, A. (2014). *Brand Media Strategy: Integrated Communications Planning in the Digital Era.* New York: Springer.

CHAPTER 3

Focus to Users

In this chapter, you will read:

1. It's not about the technology, it's about the people
2. Find your end user
3. How to enhance the user's journey?
4. People, location, and influence
5. Capturing the user's mindset
6. Develop online presence
7. Build your channels

Introduction

Today, we thrive on instant gratification. Users consume the news via 140-character tweets, watching videos instead of reading long articles, scrolling through photos or gifs, and skipping over the captions altogether. There is no shortage of user-experience lessons to be learned from this cultural shift. The only way for you to survive is to understand that no matter how much technology you have in your hands, you will always have to capture the mindset of your customer. Your customer must always be placed in the center of your online strategy.

You need to realize that your customers are having the control of your company. They always expect an immediate response to their inquiries, and of course many firms find this not only extremely annoying but also extremely difficult. Customer centricity is at the core of individualized marketing. It is rather simple to deliver highly customized messages to the consumers, but the difficulty is in being consistent across all channels.

It's Not about Technology, It's about People

It has never been only about the technology. We tend to always forget that people should be the focal point of our online strategy. The only way to succeed something like this is to move away from theories and focus on actions. The very first thing you will need to do is to listen your audience. We are not talking about just your clients, but about your overall audience. We are talking about people who could be your future clients but at the same time people who could be influencers to other potential customers.

In order for your customers to feel in control, you need to make sure to empower them with it. For example, this is applicable when you give them the choice for sign-in options or push preference centers. People are more receptive if they feel the cards are in their hands. Your customers should be able to choose via the channel they want to communicate. It is important to monitor closely the device they use as well as their behavior. By doing so, you will develop a 360-degree picture of your customer's journey and improve the buying process and create a more enhanced and beneficial journey for the customer.

If customers aren't at the center of your business, you cannot possibly begin to think about your online branding strategy. You also need to understand who your customers actually are and, more importantly, what do they care about. You need to aggregate customer information, often from multiple sources in order to get a rich customer insight. It doesn't finish there though. The second step would be for you to consider how you can effectively communicate the positive impact that your organization is having on the community. Opening an active dialogue with customers is another way you can bring customers to the center of your business.

When you engage and respond to customer service requests over social media, those customers end up spending 20 to 40 percent more money with the company. Quite simply, organizations will need to adapt or they will fail. Organizations will need a single view of the customer, deeply connected to numerous social and business platforms. That is the only way to build rich customer intelligence and insight. Business leaders will move away from the notion of "what happened" and they will start moving more and more toward predictive intelligence leveraging and advanced analytical techniques. Knowing what your customers wanted or even knowing what they want now is no longer enough. If you would like to survive in the new turbulent environment, you must now anticipate the needs of your customers.

At this point, I should clarify to you that making your business all about the customer doesn't mean that you should do what the customer wants. The customer centricity is not actually the practice of doing what your customer wants but it's actually an outcome of how you create mutual value. The evidence that you are customer centric comes from your ability to constantly change and adapt. You achieve your customer-centric outcome by creating habits that change the rhythm within your organization and also habits that change with your supporters. You need to create habits that, of course, start with understanding the customers that matter to you but also include how you prevent problems occurring for them. At the same time, you need to be able to detect problems that might occur for them and be able to differentiate your approach in a way that means something to them. In other words, you need to make them feel special.

The thing to remember is that customer-centric marketing is an ongoing process. Combining the necessary information and tools will allow you to experiment, test, and uncover what delivers the best results, as well as opportunities you may be missing. Once you know what works best, you can reproduce and expand upon specific tactics. No matter how you approach it, putting your customers at the center of your marketing strategy will help you deliver the right message at the right time through the right channel. And when the customer comes first, you'll see the impact on your profits!

Find Your End User

Another place companies fall flat when it comes to branding is in targeting their market. This has been alluded to several times, but this is because of how important it is. What's more, it's important not to fall into the common trap of presuming your target market should be "everyone" or "everyone who buys your product." While it's true that a company wants all the customers it can get, the simple fact is that "everyone" is not an achievable target market. This becomes obvious when certain large companies refuse to shift with the times. This is most visible in the television and movie industry, where the Internet has rendered the traditional business model obsolete but industries don't want to accept that. So, they cancel shows or refuse to create certain types of movies because they don't hit the market the company thinks it wants. They're afraid to market super hero merchandise to girls, as a currently visible example, and so wind up making less and less money as the traditional market segments.

When deciding on a brand's target market, it's important to get an incredibly good idea of who the end user is and, more importantly, who the end user isn't. A good example of where this goes wrong is in what's referred to as the "Triple-A games industry," which refers to large video game developing and publishing companies that create the mass market video games with budgets to rival movies. Because these video games cost so much to make, companies relentlessly focus test their products. Unfortunately, they tend to create focus groups of young males, rather than a more diverse group of gamers. The end result, which is obvious if one reads any of the video game industry news, is that many Triple-A games wind up being incredibly similar. Because of this, independent game developers had a rich market to exploit, finding groups of gamers who were not young males and in doing so carving out a permanent place for themselves. This is all to say that a company shouldn't presume what its target market is going to be. There must be a solid understanding of who the target market is supposed to be. Any company worth doing business should be able to shift focus when it turns out its product or service is more appealing to a completely different target market.

Enhance the User's Journey

What firms need to understand is that consumers nowadays are more connected than ever. With the increased use of mobile phones, they have a great amount of power. They are the ones who could decide in a matter of seconds the destiny of your brand. They are the ones who interact with your brand in the digital environment many times per day. So, what you need to do is to develop a unified and personalized marketing approach in order to make sure that you create an experience that will stay in their minds. It's the perfect time for you to step up and overdeliver. The word "overdeliver" many times sounds quite scary to most business owners. They believe that they should give things for free and hence increase their expenses. But overdeliver doesn't necessarily mean that. A business could overdeliver in many different ways and mostly through its customer service. It is of paramount importance that you ensure to create an experience for your buyers, which not only deserves but will also ultimately drives brand loyalty and marketing ROI (Return on Investment).

In order to do that, you will need to ask yourselves when does the customer journey begin. For every consumer, the customer journey starts at a different level. For some, the journey might begin once they receive your marketing message, but for some others it might start when they perform a repeat purchase as a loyal buyer. The customer's journey is the one that will ultimately create a long-term revenue. We should examine very carefully the different steps of this journey and try to use the digital technology in order to create an amazing customer experience. Let's try to analyze together some things that you should include in your digital brand in order to enhance the experience of the user's journey.

Welcome Them

The very first thing you need to do is to have a welcome program. You have worked so hard to get the e-mail of a prospect customer and you should try to make the most out of it. The reason customers are providing you with their e-mail is because they simply want to learn more about the services you are offering. It is of crucial importance that you invest in that relationship. The user's journey starts at this point. Many firms have found that a welcome program actually does the trick for their clients. You need to set up a welcome package in all of your digital platforms. In the welcome package, the future customer needs to be aware of exactly what is going to be offered to him or her. Hence, you need to provide details of what the new contact should expect from your digital marketing program. Of course, under no circumstances you should bombard the prospect with all the information at once. The messages should be broken down into pieces. You should provide a message series and each part should provide the consumer with a benefit of your brand.

At this point, you should provide the option to the visitors of your digital platform to set any type of preferences they might have in regard to future communications. Remember that the first interaction is of extreme importance. You do not want to blow this opportunity away! You need to keep in the back of your head that you should gather as much information as possible regarding your customers. If you manage to know more details about them, then your strategy is going to be more targeted and provide higher return on investment.

Constantly Connect with Them

Lead nurturing is the process of developing relationships with buyers at every stage of the sales funnel and through every step of the buyer's journey. It focuses marketing and communication efforts on listening to the needs of prospects, and providing the information and answers they need. More and more companies are all about inbound marketing, as a way for them to create more leads. Although it is becoming more and more difficult for them to do so, companies should start relying more on their inbound leads. In most cases, only a relatively small percentage of your inbound leads will be ready to make an immediate purchase, leaving upward of 90 percent of your inbound leads on the table. What you need to do is to create an effective lead nurturing strategy. By doing this, you could see an immediate impact on the results of your inbound strategy—end up with an average of 20 percent increase in sales opportunities.

The good thing is that you have some extremely sophisticated digital technology in your hands. The key here is not to be afraid to ask for help. There are many firms out there that believe they know what to do regarding their digital strategy, but they fail to do so because they don't exactly know how to implement it. Today's sophisticated digital marketing technology gives marketers the ability to deploy advanced nurture programs, allowing marketing teams to build brand preference and loyalty both before an initial sale as well as in between repeat purchases.

There are many different nurture programs that you could implement. The simplest and easiest would be to send reminder e-mails every other week. The strategy is that all people on your mailing list receive the same e-mail at the same time. The purpose of the e-mail is not about trying to sell your brand. Most of the times it should be on building the relationship with your audience. Again, that is the simplest and easiest way to keep connected. If you would like to take it to the next level, then you should try to use all the information that you have regarding your customers, in order to perform a more targeted marketing campaign. If you manage to send messages that target directly a specific customer segment, then you are in the right track!

Remind Them to Buy!

Although most companies have quite a few visitors on their websites, they don't make enough sales. Some of these companies have no idea why they don't even know at which stage of the customer journey the consumer decided not to proceed with buy. If you belong to this group, then you need to keep track of your analytics, in order to know for how long and which exact pages the consumer visited in your website. If you already know that the consumers are putting the products or services in their cart but they do not proceed to the actual buy, then you need a cart-abandonment program.

There are many companies that have not even considered of such a solution. They are putting lots of effort (time and money) into attracting the consumers and making them to want the product or service, but they just don't close the sale. The basic rule of sales always be closing (ABC) applies to online world as well! Research has shown that 67 percent of online shopping carts are abandoned before the customer completes a sale. What you need to do is to use a program that could remind your customers what they've left behind and encourage them to complete their purchase. It is a very powerful and straightforward way to reconnect with customers who navigate away from their shopping carts. It means that your company will be able to recapture sales that would have been lost and finally generate more revenue.

If you choose to use such a technique, you will be able to monitor all abandoned carts that never turned into actual orders and then deploy your marketing strategy in order to convert them. For example, you could send some personalized e-mails to those consumers and offer incentives (i.e., extra discount) in order to encourage them to complete the process. If you are selling a more complicated and technical product, then you could offer just expertise and assistance throughout the buying process.

Of course, there are some other tools, such as the browse abandonment program, that work in a very similar way. It's basically a message series that is being initiated when the visitor leaves your website without completing a conversion goal that you have set. Since these contacts may not be as far along in the buying cycle, the goal of the program is to provide helpful information to the customers and hopefully encourage them to come back to complete the purchase.

Make Them Come Back

One of the most valuable assets of the company, apart from your employees, is your customers. If they purchased from you once, you should try hard to make them repurchase. Each customer is extremely valuable to your company. It costs a lot more to try to bring new customers in than to keep your existing ones. If you manage to do that, you will convert them into loyal customers and then they will be your brand advocates in the web. Many times firms don't give the attention that is needed in such an important matter. If you haven't done so, then you need to consider implementing a loyalty program. It could be something very simple that for every three buys, they get something free or they get a discount or it might be something far more complicated. It all depends on how much money you are willing to invest to your loyalty program. Bottom line is that you need to implement a program that rewards your most loyal customers in order to strengthen even more their brand loyalty.

Of course, the following questions might pop in your mind. Who are my best customers? Are the ones who bring me more money? Are the ones who buy more often? Or are the ones who they bought more recently? There are no right or wrong answers to these questions. It all depends on the nature of your business. A way to determine your best customers could be by assessing the recency, frequency, and monetary value of their buys. As I mentioned before, it all depends on the nature of your business. For some of you, frequency could be the most important factor, whereas for some others the amount of money spent in each visit could be the most important factor. Once you have established who those customers are, you need to give them some offers that will apply only to them. A fully personalized offer will make them feel extremely special. In order to make them feel even more special, think about providing them something more than just a discount. You could offer them something like VIP access in some of your products or services. For example, they could have access to your new products first. While a simple coupon code or discount is always a nice offer, consider providing things such as early access to beta programs, VIP access at company events, or access to premium content. These small touches will go a long way in ensuring your brand is always top of mind.

Reactivate Old Customers

It is inevitable to lose some old customers. Some of them might have switched or they might just have forgotten about your brand. No matter what is the reason, customers will fall off your radar. The question is what you are going to do about it. Bottom line is that you need to reactivate them and start engaging with them more. So how will you do that? The first thing is to use your marketing research. You should use all the data you have from them in order to create personalized messages to be sent automatically. The key is to remember that each customer wants to feel special. Your optimum goal is to turn them into brand advocates. A simple solution would be to send an e-mail on a purchase anniversary. These are more likely to catch someone's eye than a generic batch-and-blast marketing message. Or, try a special promo code or discount that is delivered over a series of messages. If the customer never engages with the e-mails, consider suspending his or her name from marketing messages. Remember, it's OK to keep your database clean and full of individuals who are excited to interact with your brand! While these are just a few of the automation techniques you can use to reach your customers and prospects, getting started with these programs will ensure you're staying in touch with them during important points in the customer journey.

People, Location, and Influence

People

As we have mentioned in this chapter, it's all about the people. The customer needs to be in the center of our attention. When you think about your brand, you also need to think about who is going to buy it. You need to think not only customers' demographic variables but also their lifestyle. Lifestyle segmentation is an approach that places emphasis on the shared activities, interests, and behaviors of customers. Along with activities, lifestyle segmentation is driven by characteristics such as shared interests, opinions, attitudes and values of customers. At the same time, you need to understand their past current and future behavior. You need to target customers based on their interest or experience with your company. With this strategy, your market segments have shared familiarity with your products. Benefits sought, usage, loyalty, prospect, or customer status are common characteristics.

The digital world is a huge opportunity but at the same time is a huge challenge as well. As in the brick and wall market you need to identify, through digital this time, how you can raise awareness. Most probably you will have to use the channels that are more frequently used by your customers and start engage with them. As we discussed, at the beginning, you need to take advantage of their demographic and behavioral criteria. Since all of your customers leave a digital footprint, you should take advantage of it. First, you must understand which customers you need to look for, what type of devices they will be using, and when and at the same time which social networks, websites, and apps they engage with.

Digital branding is all about how to manage your brand in the online environment. But what if you also sell your products offline as well? In the offline environment, it is easier to manage your brand and understand the customer. For example, in retail, a customer can pick up the phone to get a location and opening hours, drive and park to the location, walk into a store, get help from staff, find their way to what they need, find a product within the price range to meet their expectations, access the checkout, purchase effectively, and leave safely and securely. All of these elements enhance their experience. The same experience should be provided in the online environment. Most of the firms out there understand this concept but there are only few firms that actually put the customer experience in the center of their strategy.

When we are talking about the element of people, we should not only think about our customers. Along with the external customer we also have the internal one. Your employees need to understand the brand promise because that is vital in order to deliver your brand properly to your external clients. From your end, you need to devote some time and money in order to recruit, educate, and train the right people. There are several reasons as to why your employees are a vital part of your online brand. For example, your customers may seek comfort online by seeing, hearing, and reading about key members of the management or customer service team.

Location

During performing offline branding one key factor is location. In other words, where your firm is going to be based, what are the demographic criteria of your target group (area that they live, language that they speak, income that they have, and so on). The problem that you will have with the variable of location in the online environment is that you will not have total control of your audiences and their location. So, what can you do? The most important aspect of online branding is that you need to adapt. Adaptation to different customer segments is the key to your success. The only way for firms to successfully sell their products across different targets (in terms of location) is to be able to culturally adapt in its market. It means that your website should be fully customized to the different needs of your target segment. That could mean different options in terms of language but to the other extreme that could also mean a totally different web design that will be more appealing to your new segment.

The only way for you to succeed is that you are fully committed to adaptation. The best international brands try to provide a unique strategy for each location. In order to be successful, you could use search engine optimization (SEO), frequency of mobile usage, and choice of operating systems to develop apps. Location as part of brand awareness and engagement has also become much more of a factor with the use of smartphones. The location is maybe one of the most difficult aspects in terms of implementation. It's the most difficult, simply because in an online environment the retailers are asked to provide a physical location. As much as we try to offer an online experience, we must face the truth! Local stores are where the most important experiences will always happen. Even the world's largest online retailers have started realizing this and have begun experimenting with pop-up physical stores. The physical experience is going to close the sale. That sale of course might not take place in the physical store but it could take place online. In those stores consumers can touch and feel a product before making a purchase, or even ask questions about the product to one of the employees. Brands that really want to stay in touch do so across all channels and not separately within each channel.

Influence

One of the most important variables that could influence your customers is the electronic word of mouth (eWOM). eWOM is an electronic interpersonal communication about products and services between consumers. Make no mistake! It is probably the most influential source of marketplace information for your consumers. The reason why it is so influential is because consumers generally tend to believe other consumers more than they believe you. It doesn't mean that they don't like your firm. They simply believe that their peers will provide them with more unbiased information.

There are a lot of product review websites (e.g., consumerreview. com), retailers' websites (e.g., amazon.com), brands' websites (e.g., forums.us.dell.com), personal blogs, message boards, and social networking sites (e.g., Facebook, MySpace) that could provide information to other peers. eWOM often occurs between people who have little or no prior relationship with one another. This anonymity allows consumers to more comfortably share their opinions without revealing their identities. The unique characteristics of eWOM encourage consumers to share their opinions with other consumers, thus increasing the volume of eWOM. As a result, there is a greater likelihood that consumers will find other consumers with product expertise on the eWOM platforms. However, the anonymous nature of eWOM can make it difficult for consumers to determine the quality and credibility of the eWOM. Determining the quality of online posts has become even more difficult now that marketers have attempted to influence eWOM by compensating consumers to review products and even going so far as to post their own reviews about their products. Because of this, consumers often look for a variety of cues when determining the quality of the online information.

Capturing the User's Mindset

A business can be marketed in many ways, but some of those options may be a waste of time for your company. For some, building a campaign is about testing the waters and trying everything once, in order to see what works best for them. That is not an effective strategy and leads to a lot of wasted money and time. You need to perform research that will show what works for your niche today so that you don't waste resources on a plan that could fail.

Digital will continue to flourish but we need to learn how to harness it. In order to do so, we need to understand the different types of technology we have in our disposal. In short, companies that chase the technological trappings of digital without first understanding whether their people have the requisite mindsets to embrace the opportunities for change and reinvention that digital brings, will likely fail. By contrast, executives who look to shape the cultures of their organizations to react quickly to emerging trends and to be open to new ways of working and thinking will be more innovative and better able to spot market shifts and thus become more profitable and disruptive competitors in their industries. That translates into new, ahead-of-the-curve products, a thriving workforce, and new industry-altering business models that can outpace the competition.

As consumers are rapidly moving between channels and platforms, marketers are finding it so difficult to implement an integrated marketing strategy. In today's highly cluttered digital marketing environment there is a great need for marketers to fully comprehend a new breed of consumers. For example, the modern consumer can check into a store with the use of a geolocation service (i.e., Foursquare, Google+, or Facebook check-in), redeem an offer that is available only for those consumers who are online, pay with Android Pay or Apple Pay, and share his or her comments on social media. Apparently, the new consumer is not simply digitalized. The new consumers have three basic characteristics: they have extremely high social media engagement, they search for local offering, and they do most things through their phones. Smartphones are empowering consumers and transforming shopping and recreational behaviors. Shopping used to be fun. Now it is much more than that. It is a game with immediate rewards and a chance to get in touch with friends and followers.

Develop Online Presence

The first thing that people do when they look for a product is to Google it. It doesn't matter if we like it or not but the Internet has changed the whole way that we search and evaluate companies. Do you know that some customers out there are looking for your products? The million-dollar question is are your products easy to find and if they are, are consumers ready to buy them? In order for that to happen, your message needs to be conveyed in a way that will convince the consumers to buy it. From your website to your social media networks, it's all about creating your online and unique "digital bang." And because the competition is fierce, your digital bang needs to be so loud that it will be very difficult to be ignored!

Of course, at the same time it's extremely important to have an end game. Basically, you need to set your priorities and targets, right from the beginning. Let's face it; today's online marketplace is more competitive than ever. You need some help from someone that not only understands the customer journey but also knows how to develop an online marketing strategy that helps your brand become known as "the best answer" wherever prospects and customers may be looking: search, social media, industry media or e-mail. You need to develop an online marketing strategy that helps create, easy to find, engaging experiences that inspire action. You should identify your business objectives, and use the right combination of digital marketing consultancy services to reach these goals. Whatever your objectives are, they should be the foundations of your digital marketing strategy.

One of the ways to establish online presence is through social media. The mistake that many firms make is that they do not have a specific marketing strategy when they use social media. It's not only about letting everybody know how great your brand is on Twitter, LinkedIn, Pinterest or Facebook. You should use social media in order to grow your customer loyalty, build value and most importantly help your business grow. Understanding your audience is key to your brand's success in social media. The buyer's journey, from discovery to conversion, may extend over weeks or months of information gathering, consumption and hopefully, sharing. You need to mix traditional marketing, search marketing, and social media to work for your brand and to improve direct website traffic, create brand buzz, and get higher search engine rankings. Your aim is to make the consumers not only to join your social network community, but also to buy your product and to refer your brand to peers and social networks.

Of course, online advertising allows brands to reach out beyond their existing networks, to tap into new, highly targeted audiences via search, social or display ads. Companies get the best ROI in social advertising through strategic planning, top quality ad creative, and ongoing campaign measurement and optimization. You should look into adding e-mail marketing to your integrated online marketing program and establish a customer-centric program geared at converting and retaining customers.

Build Your Channels Successfully

In the following chapters, we will further analyze on how you can build the proper channels in order to have a successful digital brand. There are a few points, though, that you need to take under consideration before you start. First of all, you need to have a clear vision on your branding. As in non–digital branding, the e-branding involves the tone, feel, and message that your brand gives off, whether in nonverbal visual cues or written text. It is of paramount importance that you have been very clear regarding the previous elements. The next step would be to start having an online presence. You could start building your website and have some social media presence. At this point, you need to start increasing the brand awareness.

Later, once you start having an increased brand awareness, you can invest more on your advertising campaign in order to take advantage of the momentum of your brand.

One of the most common mistakes that firms do while building their online brand is that they are not being consistent. Consistency is the most important factor when it comes to communicate your brand. Consistency could be on how many times you post and where exactly but even more what exactly are you saying. It does not matter if you post once a week or if you post everyday as long as you are being consistent. You cannot post every day in your blog for a week and then just forget about it and post again after a month. Of course, that will take lots of effort. It takes time to build authority and rapport with your audience and search engines; consistency helps you build that rapport. You also want to be consistent with where you post. Focusing on a few main digital channels like e-mail, social media, and blogging might be all you focus on. Then, when you are consistent on those, you can add other digital advertising channels. Do not over do it right at the beginning. Small steps are the key!

Another common mistake is that many times firms overdo it. There are so many brands out there that are trying hard to be heard. As a result, they spend a lot of money in advertising with a solely goal to be everywhere and eventually to be noticed. That is a very big mistake. With the use of technology, we can minimize our marketing budget and maximize each effectiveness. What we need to do is to just listen. We need to listen to the audience to understand if our message is accepted from them or not. After that, we need to listen their response. There are so many cases of firms that post on their social media accounts and then they do not even bother checking the replies/comments. That is why if you manage to engage with your audience, your firm will stick out. Of course, you need to bear in mind that everything keeps changing in the digital environment. New technologies, new generations, and new behavior trends force digital marketers to adapt or get left behind.

In a digital world that is constantly changing, marketers need to be proactive to find the latest and greatest opportunities. Those who embrace new digital channels often build stronger and more visible presences because they were there first. You can obviously wait until it's a tried and true digital channel, but you risk getting lost in the sea of marketers who have also decided to embrace this new channel. For example, brands that embraced video with YouTube from the start didn't get lost in the crowd of businesses that are now trying to use video marketing in their digital strategy. The digital marketing landscape makes it very easy for marketers to broadcast their message and be quite proactive in their marketing to consumers. Unfortunately, this means that the marketing landscape is very competitive and, sometimes, aggressive. Embracing a few key perspectives is essential for any brand to grow its business with online channels today!

Summary

By now it should be very clear to you that an online brand should be all about your customers and not about your firm. The more you engage with them, the more they are going to buy products and services from your firm. The more they buy, the more loyal they become. You can clearly understand that soon your loyal customers are going to be your advocates in the web. What you should never forget though is that customer-centric marketing is an ongoing process.

You also need to think the various levels of the customer journey begin. As we discussed in this chapter, the customer journey might start at a different level for each of your customers. What you need to do of course is to encourage them to stay "tuned" in your online platform. Bear in mind that the key is to constantly try to stay connected and remind them to buy, and last but not least make them come back to buy some more. The digital world is a huge opportunity but at the same time is a huge challenge as well. One of the most important variables that could influence your customers is the eWOM. eWOM is an electronic interpersonal communication about products and services between consumers. Make no mistake! It is probably the most influential source of marketplace information for your consumers. What you need to do is to avoid some common mistakes that most firms do. While building your online brand, you must keep a high level of consistency. Consistency could be on how many times you post, where exactly you post, and even more what exactly are you saying.

In a digital world that is constantly changing, marketers need to be proactive to find the latest and greatest opportunities. They need to take innovative technologies such as smartphones apps under consideration. These technologies empower consumers and transform shopping in a game with immediate rewards and a chance to get in touch with friends and followers.

Bibliography

Aaker, D. A., & Biel, A. (2013). *Brand Equity & Advertising: Advertising's Role in Building Strong Brands*. Psychology Press.

Benedicktus, R. L., Brady, M. K., Darke, P. R., & Voorhees, C. M. (2010). Conveying trustworthiness to online consumers: Reactions to consensus, physical store presence, brand familiarity, and generalized suspicion. *Journal of Retailing, 86*(4), 322-335.

Confos, N., Confos, N., Davis, T., & Davis, T. (2016). Young consumer-brand relationship building potential using digital marketing. *European Journal of Marketing, 50*(11), 1993-2017.

Dayal, S., Landesberg, H., & Zeisser, M. (2000). Building digital brands. *The McKinsey Quarterly*, 42-42.

Dubois, D. (2016). *Digital and Social Strategies for Luxury Brands*. Luxusmarkenmanagement: Grundlagen, Strategien und praktische Umsetzung, 327.

Gürhan-Canli, Z., Hayran, C., & Sarial-Abi, G. (2016). Customer-based brand equity in a technologically fast-paced, connected, and constrained environment. *AMS Review, 6*(1-2), 23-32.

Keller, K. L. (2016). Reflections on customer-based brand equity: perspectives, progress, and priorities. *AMS Review, 6*(1-2), 1-16.

Keller, K. L., Sternthal, B., & Tybout, A. (2002). Three questions you need to ask about your brand. *Harvard Business Review, 80*(9), 80-89.

Landa, R. (2016). Building a brand narrative in the digital age. In R. Landa (Ed.). *Advertising by Design: Generating and Designing Creative Ideas Across Media* (pp. 78-89). Hoboken: John Wiley & Sons Inc.

Malthouse, E. C., Calder, B. J., & Vandenbosch, M. (2016). Creating brand engagement on digital, social and mobile media (pp. 85-101). In R. J. Brodie, L. D. Hollebeek, & J. Conduit (Eds.). *Customer Engagement*. New York: Routledge.

Øverland, A. P. (2016). *Always on: Digital Brand Strategy in a Big Data World*. New York: Routledge.

Pike, S., Gentle, J., Kelly, L., & Beatson, A. (2016). Tracking brand positioning for an emerging destination: 2003 to 2015. *Tourism and Hospitality Research,* 1467358416646821.

Singh, J., Quamina, L. T., & Xue, M. (2017). '10 million followers and counting': How digital brand alliances between online influencers and brands impact consumer value perceptions. London: Kingston University.

Swaminathan, V. (2016). Branding in the digital era: new directions for research on customer-based brand equity. *AMS review, 6*(1-2), 33-38.

Yao, L. (2016). Position the Brand: Identify the Role of Social Media for Public Accounting Firms in Digital Age. Master's thesis, Liberty University.

CHAPTER 4

How Can I Build My Digital Brand?

In this chapter, you will read:

Introduction

Every day, it seems that the world is getting smaller. This is particularly evident in the digital marketing realm. Gone are the days when businesses could only hang up posters, send flyers, or purchase ad spots on the radio or television to get their name out in the open. In today's digital era, reaching your target audience is possible in just a few clicks.

In the early days of the World Wide Web, banner advertisements had been the go-to marketing medium for countless businesses. To this day, these ads remain prominent especially for direct response campaigns. The problem, however, is that this type of display advertising focuses primarily on short-term conversions. Ads urging online users to "click now" could be seen on virtually all websites. This strategy hardly works today, as consumers have become blind to these kinds of advertisements. But as a digital marketer, what you must understand is that the success of display advertising should not only be measured by the number of clicks you receive. Banner advertisements can now be used to formulate effective digital branding strategies.

An excellent digital brand can take any business to new heights. It can be just what you need to fuel business growth, even if you're a start-up with limited resources. Growing your digital presence enables you to target the right audience instead of shelling out money on various marketing campaigns that might not reward you with long-term gains. How your audience perceives and understands you, form the foundation of your digital branding. It is necessary to provide prospective customers with a consistent experience. This has a lot to do with your content marketing strategy.

Build a Digital Personality

Content allows your brand to develop an identity and increase visibility. There's an old adage in marketing that says, "Know your audience." Back in the day, this can prove difficult to do. You can play the guessing game of what TV time slots your target customers are most active. But in the digital era, it has become much easier to glean consumer information and create user profiles to help you develop a content creation strategy. A thorough understanding of your audience and what challenges them can mean a lot in terms of boosting your value proposition. This means going beyond demographic information including name and location. It's necessary to figure out what obstacles they face when trying to do a certain task or meeting a goal.

The next step is developing content that effectively delivers the real value in your offering. You must make sure that your content highlights how your product or service helps eliminate the challenges faced by your target audience. Consumers form an impression of your digital brand based largely on your content. It is easy to convey the mission and vision of your company, but remember that it's ultimately about the customers. Instead of simply trying to make your brand look good through a sales-oriented company profile, focus on connecting with your audience.

Content that engages potential customers in a unique and meaningful way can boost authority and credibility. The last thing you want is to look like just another company leveraging digital marketing without thinking about its customers. Place particular emphasis on telling a story that resonates with people while ensuring that your content remains consistent in appearance, feel, scope, and design across all platforms you use. The personality of your digital brand must shine through in your content. Providing consistency makes it possible for your target audience to form a memory structure, immediately thinking about your offering and the value that comes with it every time they see your brand.

The Digital Marketing Toolkit

The scope of digital marketing is wide, but there is no reason to feel overwhelmed. To cover all the bases, you need to equip yourself with useful tools that make the different processes involved much easier to execute and monitor. Of course, it helps to get your hands dirty and do some parts of the strategy manually at first. You do not want to fire up a tool and automate everything without a complete understanding of how things work. Some tools also come with a learning curve, which entails a greater time investment in addition to learning all areas of digital marketing. This shouldn't deter you, though. And if you're worried about your limited budget, then you'll be pleased to know that there are free tools that can get the job done. Most of the tools also offer free trials, and so you can test the waters first and see how much of a difference they make on your day-to-day operations. For easier reading, the tools will be categorized according to the digital marketing strategy they fall under. Note that the list comes in no particular order, as all of them must be weighed equally to develop the optimal strategy.

Social Is Personal

As of January 2017, there are 1.8 billion Facebook users, 600 million Instagram users, and 300 million Twitter users. And these are only three of the most popular social media platforms; countless others are used by your target audience, and so you can't afford to miss this enormous opportunity to cater to prospective customers.

Online users spend a lot of time on social media, making it an essential marketing channel for brands. What you should keep in mind, however, is that growing your social presence wouldn't be possible by simply sharing content. You must be proactive and socialize with your followers. Everybody knows how vocal customers can be on social media, and you can take advantage of this by creating social profiles that do not only promote your content but actively communicate with your audience.

For maximum efficiency, it's necessary to find out what social channels are used by potential customers. It can prove useless to grow your following on a certain social media platform when most of your target audience spends their time elsewhere. In most cases, though, you need to utilize multiple channels to expose your digital brand to a wider range of prospects. With several accounts to keep track of, things can easily get out of hand. But with a social media management tool, you can monitor activity across your accounts and even set up autoresponders and scheduled posts for hands-free digital branding.

Sprout Social

If you need not just a social media management tool but also an engagement platform as well, then Sprout Social should definitely sit high on your list. It's a powerful tool that makes it easier than ever to connect with current and prospective customers while building brand loyalty at the same time. One of the standout features of Sprout Social is the Smart Inbox. This feature streamlines all the messages from your social profiles into one location. This can be a huge time-saver as it enables you to focus on the messages that require the most attention. It also helps compare trends over time, such as the volume of incoming messages you receive per hour or day.

Social media can also function as an extension of your customer service. This is where Sprout's social customer relationship management tools enter the picture. You don't want to sound like a robot when responding to customer feedback. These social CRM (Customer Relationship Management) tools give access to complete conversation history as well as customer contact information, thus allowing you to respond in a timely and personal manner.

Hootsuite

Many online marketers use Hootsuite for posting regular updates to their social profiles. However, it also serves as a powerful social media management tool. The free plan is perfect for small startups, providing you with several features to manage multiple networks and grow your audience. Hootsuite makes it easier to monitor your social media marketing efforts through a single, intuitive dashboard. From here, you can access tools for managing your social profiles, analyzing follower growth, capturing leads, scheduling posts, and learning from free social media courses. Another fantastic use for Hootsuite is for tracking messages and mentions of your brand. This can positively impact your digital branding as you get alerts for conversations happening in the realm of social media involving your business.

Built-In Advertising Tools

The top social media platforms also come with their own, in-house advertising tools. While you can opt for third-party, multichannel advertising software, it's worthwhile to look into these built-in tools and try them out yourself before shelling out money. Facebook offers the Power Editor for creating and running ad campaigns on their platform. In just a few simple steps, you can get your ads shown to your target audience. It's worth noting that Facebook constantly tweaks its targeting features to help publishers get the most out of their advertising campaigns. It also has budgeting features so that you can ensure that you won't go beyond your budget when engaging in Facebook marketing.

Twitter may not have the staggering user base of Facebook, but it still pays to leverage the platform to grow your digital brand. The Twitter Native Platform offers impressive targeting features. For one, it boasts of a segmentation functionality that allows you to target particular keywords, ensuring that your ads appear for the most relevant terms.

Search Engine Optimization

The biggest sources of inbound web traffic for most websites are search engines. What makes search engine traffic special is that it can drive laser-targeted traffic to your website. That is, of course, if you manage to rank for the most relevant and profitable keywords used by prospective customers. Search engine optimization (SEO) involves the use of different techniques with the objective of showing up higher in the organic search listings. Note that it is different from search engine marketing, which deals with paid organic results.

Search engines such as Google and Bing use algorithms that take into consideration a multitude of different factors. Nobody knows what all these factors are exactly, but some are well known including keyword usage and links. With the help of SEO tools, you can set up more effective campaigns through competitive analysis, keyword research, and link building.

Google Search Console

First in the list is a free tool straight from Google. The Search Console is your one-stop shop for Google Search results data for all your online properties. With just a single account, you can link multiple domains and keep track of different metrics including rankings, impressions, and CTR (Click-through rate). With an easy-to-understand interface, you should be up and running with this tool in no time. It provides all the necessary information to help maintain your site's online presence. Aside from how well your web pages perform in terms of traffic, you can also check for web crawl errors, mobile friendliness, and page load speed. You can also submit URLs, which proves particularly useful if you want to index new or updated content on your website. Considering that this is a free service from Google, there's virtually no reason not to add your website to the Search Console.

SEMRush

It's always helpful to keep an eye out on what your competitors are doing. If they outrank you in the organic listings, you might want to take a peek into their strategy and adopt what works for your future campaigns. Sound too daunting a task? Not with SEMRush. Priding itself as an all-in-one toolkit for digital marketers, SEMRush offers a wide range of features that should help kick start your strategy. Aside from being able to monitor important site metrics and conduct a technical SEO audit, this tool lets you perform competitive analysis without breaking a sweat. An easy way to leverage the tool is to keep track of the ranking fluctuations of your competitors. You can also take a look at their backlink profile and figure out whether you can acquire links from the same sources. By identifying such opportunities, you can gain an edge and be in a better position to outrank the competition.

Moz

Over the years, Moz has become synonymous to SEO—and for good reason. The company offers products geared toward all kinds of entrepreneurs. For one, the Moz Pro gives you access to a suite of SEO tools such as a rank tracker and backlink checker. It also provides useful ideas for your content marketing needs. Moz Local is also a popular tool, thanks in large part to the increasing demand for local SEO. By simply entering your business information, Moz Local helps you get listed on the most relevant platforms such as online business directories. You might also want to subscribe to the Moz Blog. The experts over at Moz regularly share the latest news and strategies in the world of SEO, and so you can get a head start especially when a new algorithm sets in.

Ahrefs

Every SEO knows how powerful links are in terms of boosting rankings. But you should also remember that the wrong links can hurt your ranking potential. It's necessary to monitor your link profile to ensure it remains healthy and favorable in the eyes of search engine spiders. Ahrefs is a powerful backlink checker and analysis tool. It boasts of the largest backlink index; so it can return links, which other tools of its kind may miss. Ahrefs has also come up with TrustFlow and CitationFlow, two metrics that give you a quick idea of how powerful your domain is. Aside from checking the number of links pointing to your website, this tool also lets you see your referring domains and anchor text ratio. It's vital that you analyze these factors as well as they have a huge impact on your search engine rankings.

E-mail Marketing

Promoting your business through sending e-mail messages may seem outdated, but it remains an effective technique to this day. In fact, many brands continue to increase their allotted budget for e-mail marketing every year as it yields excellent returns when implemented correctly. What's great about sending e-mails is that your target customers can now view them almost instantly, thanks to the ever-growing usage of smartphones and tablets. People no longer need to turn on their desktop or laptop computer just to open their e-mail inbox. Push notifications alert your targets faster than ever.

Effective e-mail marketing can boost your digital branding, as you can send e-mails for a variety of purposes—be it to send a weekly newsletter, share your latest posts on social media, or update subscribers about discounts and promos. Even more compelling, e-mail continues to drive more e-commerce purchases compared to other marketing channels including organic search, display advertising, and social media.

If you have a large e-mail list, it can get pretty difficult to do things by hand. Let's look at a few e-mail marketing software to make the process easier.

MailChimp

Millions of people use MailChimp every day, and there are plenty of reasons why you should do so as well. It is a robust e-mail marketing platform that gives access to a variety of features to streamline your campaigns. One of the best aspects of MailChimp is its ease-of-use. The freemium plan can do the trick even for complete amateurs. With this tool, you can expect to craft fun and exciting newsletters even with zero experience in design. This makes your marketing messages stand out as you effectively grab the attention of readers with rich media instead of simply sending blocks of text.

Not only does MailChimp make sending e-mails faster and easier, but it also helps you keep track of campaign performance. You can conduct A/B testing, allowing you to send completely different e-mails to your target audience and analyze what produces optimal conversions.

Pair this with its seamless integration with some of the most popular web applications and MailChimp proves to be a must-have in your digital branding arsenal.

ConvertKit

While relatively new to the scene, ConvertKit has quickly gained traction, thanks to excellent reviews from bloggers across different industries. What immediately stands out from this e-mail marketing software is its intuitive user-interface. You shouldn't have any trouble getting started regardless of what feature you want to use. One feature ConvertKit has that other e-mail marketing tools don't is the ability to determine what pages drive list growth. You can view well-designed charts that tell you how many subscribers you get each day and what blog posts they are in at the point of conversion. And if you're planning to create web courses, ConvertKit makes the process as easy as making traditional web forms and e-mail blasts. Because it is geared toward bloggers and authors, ConvertKit also integrates with nonconventional applications and plug-ins.

Aweber

Aweber is another widely used e-mail marketing software. It proves to be one of the most cost-effective tools on the market for managing your e-mail marketing campaigns. While it is not loaded with features, it has all the basics that should be enough for most digital marketers. As with other tools of its kind, Aweber has an excellent reporting tool that lets you see what techniques work and what doesn't. It also has a user-friendly e-mail campaign creator, guiding you through the step-by-step process of creating signup forms and newsletters. Aweber also integrates with a host of third-party applications, perhaps the most notable of which is Word-Press. In just a single click, you can set up an e-mail signup form on your website. This tool also allows you to conduct split testing so that you can send out variations of your marketing messages and optimize for better open and engagement rates.

Display Retargeting

Have you ever experienced browsing a product in an online marketplace and not pushing through with the purchase, only to get followed by an ad for that same product no matter where you go on the web? This is display retargeting in action. Imagine how powerful this is for your digital branding efforts. By using the right channels and segmenting your audience carefully, you can create memory structures among your target customers that build your credibility over time.

Audience retargeting has become more powerful over the past few years. Today, it's easy to segment your audience not only based on demographic information, but also on more specific factors such as gender, interest, employment, and civil status. For instance, it's entirely possible to target first-time parents in New York through proper audience retargeting.

This technique enables you to reach prospects that have already shown interest in your offering. You can target those who have searched for your brand, visited your website, or opened your e-mail marketing message. Retargeting has the ability to convert somebody with little exposure to your brand into a loyal brand advocate.

This heightened efficiency of audience segmentation can be a driving factor for increasing the reach of your digital brand. But if you're completely new to the concept, it's recommended to use tools and enlist the services of experts to get you started in the right direction.

AdRoll

In the retargeting field, AdRoll continues to be one of the most prominent names. More than 30,000 brands use the platform to gain higher visibility on different online marketing platforms. By joining AdRoll, you get access to over 500 ad exchanges. This includes the top social media sites like Facebook, Instagram, and Twitter.

The real power of AdRoll, however, lies in its ability to display ads in high-converting spots. You can monitor the performance of your ads and tweak your campaigns using their simple platform. They also employ a real-time bidding algorithm called BidIQ, which ensures that you pay the right amount in exchange for the right ad placement.

ReTargeter

ReTargeter promises to provide digital advertising solutions to reach your audience regardless of where they are on the web. Established in 2009, ReTargeter has been at the forefront of the programmatic advertising space ever since. Its primary goal is to help serve your display ads to the right audience at the right time. It's interesting to note that Sellpoints, a company that specializes in e-commerce, acquired ReTargeter in 2015. This has made the platform even more powerful, with access to consumer behavioral data. Leveraging this data enabled ReTargeter to enhance their predictive analytics capabilities, which translates to higher converting retargeting and prospecting campaigns for your digital brand. If you're familiar with retargeting techniques, you can use it as a self-service platform. Otherwise, you can let their team of retargeting experts handle everything for you.

Google AdWords Retargeting

Google uses the term remarketing, but it refers to the same concept. This should be your go-to platform if you want to show ads to prospects who have visited your website or accessed your mobile application. It helps you to easily reconnect with someone who didn't convert the first time, opening new doors for better conversions and higher profits in the long term. What's amazing about remarketing with Google AdWords is that you get to choose exactly what platforms to utilize for your campaigns. Standard and dynamic marketing shows your ads to visitors surfing Display Network websites. If you want your ads to be shown to users who've used your app while they access other apps, then remarketing for mobile apps does just that. You can also use video remarketing, e-mail-list remarketing, and search ads remarketing.

Affiliate Marketing

It is often said that word of mouth is the best form of marketing. In the digital world, however, this can be a little tricky. How can you get other people to recommend your offering to others? One way is through leveraging the power of affiliate marketing. This method revolves around the idea of getting people to become brand advocates while paying them a percentage of every sale they make.

Recent studies show that consumers treat online recommendations the same way as suggestions from people they know in real life. This can enhance your digital branding as the more people talk about and recommend your brand, the more prospective customers learn to trust and value your offering. Some businesses decide to set up their own affiliate marketing program. If you're a start-up, however, this can be too complicated. Joining affiliate marketing networks serves as an excellent alternative. This gives you access to an enormous network of publishers who are ready and willing to promote your brand to their laser-targeted traffic.

Commission Junction

One of the most popular affiliate marketing platforms for advertisers is Commission Junction. For many years, it has established its reputation in the industry, thanks in large part to its vast network of bloggers. Commission Junction understands full well that the consumer journey has changed over the years. With the increasing popularity of online shopping, consumers have gotten way smarter when it comes to weeding out bad products from their list. Through affiliate marketing, however, it's possible to influence their purchasing decision by tapping publishers and letting them promote your offering. The platform comes with advertising tools to help optimize your campaigns. From a well-designed dashboard to easy-to-understand graphs and charts, you can expect these tools to be comprehensive enough in providing you with the most crucial performance metrics. With nearly two decades of experience under their belt, you can bet that the experts over at Commission Junction know their stuff. They also use the most advanced techniques to organize advertisers and publishers in their network, ensuring that optimal returns are enjoyed by both parties.

VigLink

VigLink has an interesting take on affiliate marketing. It uses content from publishers and places revenue generating hyperlinks in the most relevant places. With more online users growing blind to banner advertisements, using contextual links can lead to higher conversion rates. Regardless of your digital branding goals, you can certainly find a use for VigLink. It is one of the most reputable content networks today, boasting of more than 60,000 advertisers. Their large network of publishers ensures that there will always be content that's timely, engaging and relevant for your particular niche. By partnering with VigLink, you can find influential publishers across a variety of industries including travel, fashion, technology, and more.

CAKE

Using multiple affiliate networks can get confusing real quick, and so it's nice to have a comprehensive management tool to help keep track of everything. CAKE is an excellent tool to help resolve this dilemma. This cloud-based tool proves to be a huge time-saver. Upon accessing the all-in-one dashboard, you'll immediately realize how easy to use this tool really is. Aside from just monitoring how well your ads perform on different networks, CAKE also has handy features for managing contacts and reviewing metrics in real-time. CAKE can also help you save money on ad spend by effectively targeting ads and gathering insight into the journey of prospective customers. This intelligence data makes it easy to optimize your affiliate marketing campaigns, eliminate nonperforming ads, and boost efforts that best lead to conversions.

Content Marketing

You already know that content can make or break your digital branding campaigns. It doesn't matter how much traffic your website gets, how many subscribers you have in your e-mail list, or how large of a following you have on social media if you fail to deliver content that engages and connects with potential customers. It's also worth understanding that online users have become largely visual, meaning they prefer consuming content with incorporated rich media. Posts that only contain blocks of text may no longer work as great as it used to. For this reason, you must learn to look beyond traditional blog posts and consider other content formats to determine what best engages your target audience.

Content Creation

For any shot at succeeding, you must have a steady supply of content to feed all the marketing channels you use. You need written content for your blog, high-quality images for driving engagement rates, and perhaps even videos if your customers would find value in them. You may also want to consider infographics, GIFs, podcasts, and live streaming.

With a variety of formats to choose from, there's a good chance you do not have enough time to do everything from scratch. To help boost your content creation strategy, here are some useful tools to add to your toolkit.

Canva

This cloud-based design tool is highly popular among brands looking for high-quality images to be shared on blogs, social platforms, and other marketing channels. You can start with their free version, which already gives access to a ton of images across different categories. With Canva, you can create captivating and unique photos even without prior experience. It's all a matter of picking an image and using its simple editor to make tweaks to the photo.

For instance, adding a caption is as easy as hitting the text box and typing your desired message. There are also premade templates to help you come up with outstanding designs. It doesn't matter if you're not the artistic type. Canva does the heavy lifting for you, as you're left with simple enhancements to make the photos your own.

Visual.ly

If you do not have the time, interest, or skills to produce your own visual content, then you might want to look into Visual.ly. This platform connects advertisers in need of visual content to those who have the skills to produce it. In a few simple steps, you can get your hands on high-quality, custom-designed rich media ready to be shared on your chosen marketing platforms. Visual.ly has a streamlined process to get the job done in the most efficient fashion. You only need to describe your project, explain what you want to achieve with the visual content, and pick what format you need for your campaign. After these steps, you will be given a quote for the project. Upon accepting the quote, Visual.ly will pair you with the best fit according to your particular needs. With more than 1,000 writers, animators, and designers, you can rest assured that their team can do a fantastic job building your digital brand through effective content.

Contently

For an all-in-one content marketing solution, Contently makes a strong case to be your go-to resource. This award-winning content marketing software has everything you need to manage all your campaigns, track performance, and optimize using innovative technology. Contently offers tools that streamline the process of content creation. You will be guided from the ideation process all the way to the distribution of your content. What's more amazing is that it enables you to transform ordinary blog posts into interactive multimedia projects with which your target audience will surely resonate.

The software also has the ability to match you with the right content creator depending on your content requirements. The platform boasts of a network consisting of over 100,000 freelancers. They can also publish your content on your social profiles, blogs, and e-mail so that you can save precious time. Contently also provides granular content data that allows you to come up with informed decisions regarding your content marketing strategy. Determine what works and eliminate what doesn't to optimize your campaigns.

Content Curation

This technique basically involves sharing content from other credible sources in your niche. It's a perfect way to fill your content calendar, especially if you need to keep engagement up while running low on content you create yourself. But why should you even consider sharing content other than your own? Content Curation works because it establishes authority. When your target audience sees that you're willing to share posts from other authoritative sources, even from businesses that may compete with your offering, it shows that you are not all about making money. You can avoid looking too salesy by exposing your prospects to other kinds of content. This also shows that you are keeping up with the latest news and trends in the industry, boosting your credibility even further.

Google Alerts

It's unfortunate that Google Alerts do not get as much attention as it deserves. This tool is simple yet very powerful, allowing you to keep track and get notifications for the most relevant keywords to your business. What's great about Google Alerts is that you can set it up only one time and benefit from it for months or even years to come. You can use keywords related to your business or those to your competitors. That way, you can instantly get notified when new posts are published about the keywords you monitor.

Feedly

If blog content is the primary format you want to share, then Feedly is a must-have tool. This online resource makes it straightforward to curate blog content from a variety of sources. You get to choose from a wide range of blogs and publications, giving you access to the most recent topics that you can share or use as topic inspirations. The well-laid out interface of Feedly makes it a pleasure to use. It's easy to organize all the blog content you want to monitor. The tool also provides a minimalist reading experience, designed specifically for maximum productivity. Feedly also integrates with third-party applications such as Sprout Social; so you can share your chosen blogs continuously with minimal manual intervention.

Scoop.it

Scoop.it works pretty much the same way as other Content Curation tools on the market, but it sets itself apart with its advanced content marketing automation features. Using this tool, you can grow your digital presence by publishing high-quality content based on your keywords of choice. Simply enter your keyword list and discover an endless amount of content for you to share on your social channels or blog. You also have the option of adding perspective to the curated content before publishing or distributing to your desired platforms.

Scoop.it also highlights its content marketing automation tools. These allow you to create better content by delving into useful customer information. You can also research about what kind of content and keywords resonate best with your target audience using actual content and performance metrics published on the web. There is also a smart calendar that lets you visualize your content marketing plan. You can schedule posts and promote content in just a few clicks. You can also measure ROI (Return on Investment) with its built-in analytics tool.

Quora

For online users seeking answers to their questions, the go-to platform is Quora. This website is where you can glean authoritative answers to and opinions about pretty much anything under the sun. Using Quora allows you to determine what questions potential customers have in mind, ones a keyword research tool will often fail to provide. By knowing these questions and challenges, you can come up with content ideas that thoroughly satisfy the queries of your target audience. You can also explore the hottest topics surrounding your field. Creating content based on authoritative answers can drive more traffic and better engagement to your blog. It's also possible to get notified about new posts relevant to your niche, and so you always have something to turn to when your content idea tank runs empty.

Website Analytics

One of the primary advantages of digital marketing over traditional marketing methods is that it gives you a much clearer picture of the results you get from running your campaigns. Many beginners in digital marketing, however, do not know how to utilize this data to their advantage. While you can be successful without giving the slightest attention to metrics such as time on page, number of pages per visit, and bounce rate, you can set up more effective campaigns by doing so. This is because these site metrics help you piece together a picture of how visitors use your website, consume your content, and follow through with your desired call to action.

The process can sound intimidating at first, but once you get the hang of it, you will surely make more data-driven marketing initiatives. Knowing your audience plays a key role in your overall marketing strategy, you must take a proactive approach to ensure that you're always on top of your site performance and consumer behavior.

The following website analytics tools should help you set up more fine-tuned user profiles by providing insightful customer information.

Google Analytics

Once again, Google has a free offering for webmasters who want to keep track of different site metrics. By simply adding your domain, this tool gives you access to a ton of different features that let you have a better understanding of how visitors navigate your website.

There is a multitude of different metrics you can monitor, each of which helps in knowing your audience better. But if you only have so much time to keep track of a few, be sure they are bounce rate, conversion rate, and channels. A bounce is counted when a visitor lands on your site, visits a single page, and then leaves your website without completing any other action. In general, you do not want to see a high bounce rate on your web pages as this indicates poor content and user experience. The first step to improving bounce rate is to conduct a full site audit, determining what the cause of the problem is. See whether visitors are leaving because of your content, slow page load speed, or terrible user experience.

Conversion rate is an excellent metric for showing how successful you are at compelling users to do what you want them to accomplish. This reflects the number of online visitors who turn into leads after performing a specific action on your page. High traffic proves useless if conversions are low. In such a case, you may want to evaluate whether you have the right content with keywords that come with high commercial intent. Channels tell you where your online visitors are coming from. You'll get to see how much of your traffic comes from social, organic search, paid search, referral, and direct sources. This gives you an idea about how effective your marketing strategies are. For instance, if you were using SEO to attract more targeted traffic, you'd want to see organic search to generate most of your site traffic.

Kissmetrics

You'll be hard pressed to find another conversion optimization tool as great as Kissmetrics. The company prides itself on using behavioral analytics to boost conversion rates. This can be just what you need to enter the mind of your target audience and come up with the optimal strategy to make them convert into qualified sales leads. Kissmetrics does its magic by mapping the entire journey of visitors on your website. From the moment visitors land on your page all the way to making a purchase, the platform helps provide useful information that allows you to fine-tune your sales funnel. Other than increasing conversions, Kissmetrics also gives suggestions on how to drive customer retention. You'll be provided with metrics that help you understand what makes leads trust your brand and what compels them to choose you over the competition. With Kissmetrics, you can align your business objectives with consumer behavior to enjoy optimal conversions.

Mention

Wouldn't it be nice to have the ability to monitor all mentions of your brand across the web? This is exactly what Mention can do for you. This innovative tool keeps you updated about all mentions of your brand online—be it on blogs or social media. There are plenty of ways to leverage this powerful media-monitoring tool. By staying informed of every instance of your brand name on the web, you can join discussions in real-time and connect with your audience instantly. You can also get notified of relevant topics in your niche, providing even more opportunities to find and interact with prospective customers.

Setting up Mention is as easy as picking what keywords you want to create alerts for. This includes your brand name. Now, the great thing about the tool is that you can rest assured that you won't get notified of irrelevant instances of your brand name or keywords. When people start talking about and sharing your brand across various online platforms, that's when you know you're gaining traction. Mention can say a lot about how well your digital branding efforts are doing.

Website Testing

When building a website, it's always tempting to take the "set-it-and-forget-it" approach. After all, you might be juggling a lot of other things in your hands, leaving you with no time to introduce changes and see their impact on your site in terms of performance. For promoting digital branding, however, you must realize that even a slight change in a single design element can spell the difference between someone clicking on the "buy now" button, and leaving your site to head elsewhere. Now, this doesn't mean you need to start completely from scratch every time you want to test something out. You also do not need any coding skills or experience in web design.

With the help of some tools, you can create beautiful landing pages quickly and compare their performance against that of your current design. You might surprise yourself after learning that simply changing the color of your anchor texts, the placement of your buttons, or the copy on your call-to-actions can significantly boost your conversion rates.

Unbounce

If you want to quickly build or tweak landing pages, Unbounce is definitely a must-try. The concept behind the tool is very simple, but it can lead to significant changes to your site especially in terms of conversions. What makes Unbounce such a special tool is that it allows users to easily build beautiful landing pages. Even if you're starting from scratch and have no web design experience, you shouldn't have any problem using the tool to come up with amazing landing pages, which you can test right away.

There is also a plethora of premade landing page and overlay templates. This should be of tremendous help especially for people who do not have the time or skills to create one from scratch. You just need to use the editor to make the necessary changes and in just a few minutes, everything's ready for split testing. After having fun with the drag and drop builder, it's time to boost conversions by thoroughly experimenting with different landing pages and convertibles. Researching on the psychology behind web design can help you decide what kinds of changes to try on your site, which could help bring in more targeted traffic and convert them into real customers.

Optimizely

The ultimate goal of Optimizely is to help your brand deliver a personalized digital experience for your customers. This is achieved through its content creation and targeting tools. This combination enables you to produce engaging content and deliver it to the right audience while eliminating the guesswork involved. The company highlights the need for digital marketers to keep up with the nonstop shifts in consumer behavior. With Optimizely, you can generate higher returns from your existing traffic without shelling out more for ad spend. It also helps to craft content that connects with customers, providing them with compelling experiences to keep bounce rates to a minimum and increase time on site. Using Optimizely gives you the chance to experiment with different kinds of experiences across all marketing channels and devices. Through this, you can better focus your resources to what areas of your marketing strategy yield the best returns.

Summary

Building your digital brand provides the avenue for increased traffic, better credibility, and higher conversions. It is high time to offer your customers a consistent and personalized digital experience, as this is a strong driving factor for brand lift. Creating such a digital presence, however, can be time-intensive and costly. But by equipping yourself with must-have digital marketing tools, you should be able to meet your business goals faster than you initially thought. You don't have to play around with all of these tools simultaneously. In fact, it is much better to focus on one area of digital marketing first before moving on to another. Do not be afraid to test things out yourself first without using tools, as this can give you better ideas on how to leverage them when it comes time to fill your marketing toolkit.

Budget constraints can also hinder you from checking out some of the tools. The good news is that most companies offer free trials so that you can test them out and decide later whether to upgrade to a paid plan. Remember to look beyond the upfront cost and factor in the potential long-term gains. If you find that the cost of the tools proves worth it for the amount of time you save, there's no reason not to push through with this business investment.

Lastly, do not forget that tools are only as effective as how you use them. They cannot magically increase your digital branding after just a few clicks of your mouse. It's actually possible to damage your branding if you fail to take the time to learn how to use the tools properly.

Given the diverse mix of free and paid tools available, building your digital brand has never been more fun. Start formulating your digital marketing strategy with the aid of these tools to improve your online presence, drive more targeted leads, and ultimately increase your bottom line. Before you know it, you have created a strong digital brand that reflects authority and credibility.

Bibliography

Andersen, S. E., & Johansen, T. S. (2016). Cause-related marketing 2.0: Connection, collaboration and commitment. *Journal of Marketing Communications, 22*(5), 524-543.

Aufreiter, N., Boudet, J., & Weng, V. (2014). Why marketers should keep sending you e-mails. *McKinsey & Company.*

Berman, R., & Katona, Z. (2013). The role of search engine optimization in search marketing. *Marketing Science, 32*(4), 644-651.

Bleier, A., & Eisenbeiss, M. (2015). Personalized online advertising effectiveness: The interplay of what, when, and where. *Marketing Science, 34*(5), 669-688.

Chang, S., & Morimoto, M. (2011). Electronic marketing communications: an evolving environment, but similar story regarding the perception of unsolicited commercial e-mail and postal direct mail. *Journal of Promotion Management, 17*(3), 360-376.

Copulsky, J., Bergstrom, A., & Simone, M. (2016). One tweak at a time: How analytics improved our content marketing. *Applied Marketing Analytics, 2*(3), 201-212.

Gupta, R., Kumar, B., & Banga, G. (2017). Role of affiliate marketing in today's era: A review. *Indian Journal of Economics and Development, 13*(2a), 687-690.

Hartemo, M., & Hartemo, M. (2016). Email marketing in the era of the empowered consumer. *Journal of Research in Interactive Marketing, 10*(3), 212-230.

Hoban, P. R., & Bucklin, R. E. (2015). Effects of internet display advertising in the purchase funnel: Model-based insights from a randomized field experiment. *Journal of Marketing Research, 52*(3), 375-393.

Järvinen, J., & Taiminen, H. (2016). Harnessing marketing automation for B2B content marketing. *Industrial Marketing Management, 54,* 164-175.

Ledford, J. L. (2015). *Search Engine Optimization Bible* (Vol. 584). Indianapolis: John Wiley & Sons.

Lewis, R. A., & Rao, J. M. (2015). The unfavorable economics of measuring the returns to advertising. *The Quarterly Journal of Economics,* qjv023.

Patil Swati, P., Pawar, B. V., & Patil Ajay, S. (2013). Search engine optimization: A Study. *Research Journal of Computer and Information Technology Sciences, 1*(1), 10-13.

Shih, B. Y., Chen, C. Y., & Chen, Z. S. (2013). An empirical study of an internet marketing strategy for search engine optimization. *Human Factors and Ergonomics in Manufacturing & Service Industries, 23*(6), 528-540.

Yu, S., Hudders, L., & Cauberghe, V. (2017). Tracking the Luxury Consumer Online: An Experimental Study on the Effectiveness of Site and Search Retargeting for Luxury Brands in China and the Netherlands: An Abstract. In *Marketing at the Confluence between Entertainment and Analytics* (pp. 1541-1541). Cham: Springer.

CHAPTER 5

Become a New Top Digital Brand

In this chapter, you will read:

1. Digital marketing doesn't work as it used to be
2. Build your brand online
3. E-branding on social media and review sites
4. Buying followers, is it worth it?

Introduction

Everyone dreams of making money on the Internet. Whether it is a huge, sprawling corporation or a small brick and wall shop that wants to expand to an online market, the Internet is a new frontier of promise and opportunity. Or at least, it was around 20 years ago. There is still plenty of opportunity on the World Wide Web. The problem is that the Wild West days of the web are long gone. For example, multiple Internet search engines such as Lycos, AskJeeves, and eventually even Yahoo fell to the onslaught of Google. These days, Google's throne is so secure that not even Microsoft, which alongside Apple is essentially the entire tech industry, can't even make headway against them.

The old websites were used to present reading material and nothing else. Soon that changed with the new type of technologies. Everything was quickly overtaken by Web 2.0. That was not all Web 2.0 changed, however. It was not some kind of software or tech upgrade, but an entirely new way for people to use the Internet. Web 2.0 is used to describe the "second evolution" of the Internet, the time in which people could respond directly to websites and have their comments remain online until the websites' servers were down. This changed the fundamental nature of the Internet from passive information into a place for active social engagement on a global scale. This is all to explain that the Internet as it exists now is entirely different from the Internet as it once existed. Yet not every business gets this basic fact. Many companies still treat the Internet as if it is the era of e-branding, in which they apply the traditional newspaper and magazine style marketing to the Internet. Needless to say, this doesn't work anymore.

Digital Marketing Doesn't Work as It Used to Be

Still a lot of companies avoid the Internet all together, recalling the Dot Com bubble bursting back in the early 2000s. Everyone was so excited for the various business opportunities the Internet offered that companies were throwing all the money they had at new Internet opportunities. Like all bubbles, it burst and left many people completely penniless. These days, the Internet works at the breakneck speed of instant gratification. Social media websites like Facebook and Twitter offer immediate social contact, YouTube offers hours of free entertainment, and there is always a live feed streaming something that is happening at right that moment somewhere in the world. This means that any company trying to use the old, traditional methods of digital marketing quickly find themselves drowning in the rapids.

The new digital technology, perhaps now in its teenage phase, has stabilized enough to allow large companies to carve out entire kingdoms but at the cost of being able to find any consistent way to market. Companies have to move at the same breakneck speed as the new technologies that are used in on the online environment, which means they have to be constantly on top of anything that is becoming popular. Because if a company doesn't get noticed immediately, it is unlikely to get noticed at all. That said, by reading this chapter, you should be able to make use of some generalized tools that could help your business. None of them are 100 percent effective, but then again, no marketing tool is 100 percent effective. Unlike traditional marketing, however, current digital marketing tools have to be upgraded and utilized constantly. What are these tools? Where did they come from? How can they best be used and how do they differ from traditional marketing? These are all questions that have no specific answer; everything depends on the type of business you are in. If you manage to answer those questions, you will become a top digital brand.

Digital branding tools change quickly, and this is especially true when new technologies are involved. If this is ever in question, go to AskJeeves and do a search on Geocities. After typing those terms into Google, it becomes obvious how quickly and completely the Internet can change. This is why any attempt to engage in e-branding first requires research. Unfortunately, even that isn't easy. Any research on digital marketing tools is going to bring up search engine optimization (SEO). This often leads companies just dipping their toe into online business to presume that SEO is all they need. Not only is that untrue, it is potentially fatal to the continued health of the company! This is because SEO is just one e-branding tool out of many. It is a useful one, and even necessary for many businesses. Yet just because it is a useful tool doesn't mean it is going to be the thing a particular company needs. What's more, there are some businesses that benefit far more from other e-branding tools than they do SEO.

This is the first, and major, way that e-branding differs from traditional marketing. Traditional marketing attempts to identify target markets and create an ad campaign that appeals to that target. It is often a good idea to run different styles of advertisements in different areas, because a target market might have different desires and needs in one area than another. If McTully wants to market its cafe style drinks, it's unlikely to create an advertisement showcasing someone drinking a mocha latte in a warm, cozy environment in Arizona or New Mexico. In that area, it might instead create an ad campaign around someone strolling through the city in summer clothes while carrying an iced coffee. Both are advertising the same thing, McTully's cafe style drinks. Yet they're targeted to different markets. Sometimes they do it the opposite way, finding a target market such as "20-year-old man" and then finding out what that market wants in each area of the country. Either way, traditional marketing allows for the creation of multiple advertisements, any of which may never be seen by people outside of the target market depending on the context.

E-branding doesn't have that luxury. When something is on the Internet, it is there forever and for everyone. Since it is impossible to market multiple target markets in the same ad campaign outside of some specific contexts (some markets are simply going to have opposing needs), you need to get clever. Instead of trying to tie marketing to an area or a specific market, you need to rely on what is popular. The different ways to do that are the different digital branding tools. This is why not every digital branding tool is beneficial to every business. Because Internet is global and there are a never-ending number of ways people are getting in touch with each other. Each of those communication methods creates a website where those people congregate. And those websites are the places where digital branding happens.

Sadly, so many businesses fail here, at this spot. They know they need to market online, but they don't realize how important it is for them to have a solid brand. Branding is everything on the Internet, and a company is known by how interesting and visible it manages to be.

Build Your Brand Online

It is easy to think that a company's brand is obvious. Sadly, that is rarely the case. It is easy for a company to think it has an obvious brand, given that the people in charge of marketing work for the company. They spend their work hours inside company property, doing company work and dealing with company business. When a person spends so much of his or her time immersed in the company, it is easy to presume everyone can see what that person sees. This is a mistake you should avoid doing. This is why branding is the first step to e-branding. Like all marketing activities, it is important to figure out what type of markets you should be targeting. For example, a comic book and collectibles shops might want to market themselves as being for people who like DC Comics rather than Marvel Comics. So, while a company may not be able to target an area market, as well as it once could, it can brand itself as for all people who fit a specific niche.

The other reason e-branding is so important is simple functionality. A website is created to generate leads and sales. If it is not catching people's notice and getting them to buy the products, then it is not doing the job it was designed to do. Unfortunately, the Internet is all about instant gratification. As mentioned previously, if a company doesn't catch people's attention quickly, the users will move on and the company will be left behind. So, what can be done to help branding? Branding has to happen internally rather than externally. Simply attempting to get the users to notice a company logo just won't cut it because there is no reason for people to pay attention to a company logo.

So, if branding is the goal, keep in mind this simple rule of thumb "Proper branding makes people remember a company fondly." There are several ways to do this, and each one is important. Some companies won't need to work on some aspects of branding while others will need to work on some aspects even harder, but these are the things to keep in mind when branding is the goal.

Brand Voice

The voice of a brand is the way the company presents itself. In the previous example, we have one comic book company to be more appealing over the other, but a brand's voice is even more in depth than that. It is not just about who the brand appeals to, it is about the way in which a company appeals to those people. To keep with the comic book example, how does the company feel about Marvel Comics? Obviously, the answer is "a company is not a person and so has no opinion," but that is not true in the case of building a brand. Maybe the company thinks Marvel comics is great, but DC Comics is better. Perhaps the company thinks Marvel comics isn't even worth reading. Perhaps the company would like to ignore the existence of Marvel comics altogether.

The brand's voice doesn't have to make grand declarations every other day, of course. In point of fact, the voice should never be a conscious thing for the reader. Rather, the reader should be able to get a sense of how the company feels in its promotional material and information presentation. This is the exact opposite of traditional marketing, in which a company may have policies but it rarely has to deal with having a particular voice one way or another. While this may be the case with online businesses (it will quickly become obvious if an online shop only sells one type of comic book), there are hundreds of other online shops that all do the exact same thing. Since there is only so much a company can do with traditional sales tactics such as temporary price drops, a brand's voice gives a user a reason to shop at one company over another. The users simply like the way that company presents itself.

White and Black Hat Tactics

Yet the one thing that remains constant is that Google works hard to ensure its search engine brings the most relevant websites to the top of the page. It does this so well, in fact, that over 90 percent of searchers don't go past the first page. As if that was not hard enough, a full 50 percent find what they're looking for with one of the first three links. The answer is clear. If a company wants to be noticed, that company needs to be on the first page for any keyword search. If possible, a company should aim for the first three links. There are two styles of digital tactics, referred to as White Hat and Black Hat tactics. As suggested by the names, White Hat tactics are designed to create the most relevant information in order to attract return users with the idea that return users are more likely to be customers. Black Hat tactics are designed to get as many eyes on the website as possible, in the hope that a larger pool of people means an increase in sales.

The most obvious way to get Google's attention is via keyword use. Keyword is a term that refers to specific words and phrases that match the search terms users are searching for. An easy example is the phrase "plumbers in Chicago." A person who needs a plumber and lives in Chicago is liable to pull out his or her phone or tablet, go to Google, and type in that very phrase. If a website has that phrase in the text, then Google's algorithm views it as relevant. Yet even though it is relevant, it has to compete with hundreds, if not thousands, of websites that have the exact same phrase.

An example of a Black Hat tactic, one that Google has recently managed to fight against, is called Keyword Stuffing. This refers to putting the keyword into a website as often as possible. The higher the number of keywords, the more relevant the Google algorithm would decide it was. A common White Hat tactic is creating multiple pages of relevant, if simple, content, which uses the keyword a more reasonable number of times. In each case, the goal is to use as many different versions of the keyword as possible. "Chicago plumbers" is only one keyword that might be used. There is also "emergency Chicago plumber," "cheap plumber Chicago," and so on.

Another thing the Google algorithm looks for is how long a person remains active on a website and how often people return to the same website. The longer and more often, the more relevant Google presumes the website is. Because so many people use the website and use it for so long when they do, it simply must be an incredibly relevant site. There are a number of different ways to use links in order to build relevancy. An example of a Black Hat tactic is the use of hidden links. These are links hidden among the text of a site, usually by making the hyperlink color the same as the normal text color, causing the user to accidentally click on them. They often cause a small user message to pop up, asking if the user would like to leave the website so that the company can claim innocence. Yet it is done on purpose, because when the message pops up, users are likely to click in surprise, thinking that something is going wrong.

Backlinks are a great White Hat tactic. These days, websites have multiple pages no matter what they are for. Not only is this encouraged, but it is necessary in order to responsibly use keywords. On these pages, it is often possible to link to other pages on the same website. This encourages users to click on these links and see the other pages. Some sites do not benefit from this as well as others, of course. An industry giant like Cracked.com makes constant use of backlinks, whereas a local pawn shop makes limited use of backlinks.

These are just a few Black and White hat tactics. You should be familiar with some of them but at the end of the day you should leave that aspect of your business to a specialist. Google will often release code for HTML and other website programming language to better craft a website to meet relevancy standards. These updates allow websites to do things such as tag context words so that Google's algorithm can recognize more than just keyword use and other programming tweaks that help companies get a step up. However, these are programming tools and are only used to enhance what digital tactics have already utilized rather than tools in and of themselves.

E-branding on Social Media and Review Sites

The next major tool for e-branding is social media marketing. As mentioned earlier, Web 2.0 took the Internet by storm. If the modern Internet has a new, fancy name then it would have to be the Social Media Age. The number of different social media websites seems to change on a daily basis. However, the social media website business has the same problem as the Internet as a whole. Namely, large companies have already carved out stable niches for themselves, making it harder to get a foot in the door. This became obvious when Google attempted to create a social media site that would do what Facebook did, but better. As anyone who pays attention noticed, Google+ quickly became obsolete. Because Google is an industry giant, the company still maintains Google+. Yet even so, it is obvious to everyone that the site is nearly useless at best.

The point is if Google can't rival Facebook then no one can. The reason people get confused about this fact is that multiple social media websites have become huge. Almost everyone has a Twitter account, as well as an Instagram account and possibly even a Tumblr account. There are also sites such as LinkedIn, and a wide array of different message boards and forums where people still discuss things and engage in active conversation. However, these websites all do different things. Facebook is a site built around the idea of a person having a single "base of operations," at least in terms of online communication. Facebook gives each user a place to post his or her thoughts, images, videos, and other media and information, which is then sent out to all the people who want to see that information. Twitter seems similar on the surface, with people following an individual and reading that individual's thoughts, videos, and images, but Twitter is designed for short bursts of information. It is limited to 140 characters, which simply is not designed for in-depth conversation. While that doesn't stop some people from trying, by and large, Twitter is designed for quick communication of simple thoughts, whereas Facebook is designed to give more information.

It is the differences between these social media websites that allow all of them to maintain their hold on the industry at the same time. Because they are all different methods of communication, people will often have accounts with all of them. That is why any company that wants to be a top brand will quickly learn what social media websites are and are not useful for its needs.

Branding on Facebook

As mentioned previously, Facebook is a website allowing the quick communication of more important and larger amounts of information. A user will post things on his or her wall (Facebook's name for a user page), which other people will read and comment on. Because Facebook allows for so many characters in a post, this makes it a good platform for the communication of nuance. That is not all Facebook does, however. Facebook also provides groups, which work in a similar way to forums. The administrator, in this case the person who set up the group and anyone they choose to give equal editing power to, creates a page based on the group's intent. If it is a fan group for a particular band, then the admin might upload photographs and promotional images of the band into the photo section. The group might upload videos of the band in the video section, allowing people to see and hear the band's music.

Facebook is a great place for any company wanting to build a loyal fan base. It allows the company to share promotional information and give its fans and customers a place to chat. Not only that, but a well-run Facebook page could be used as another way for customers to send information to the company. There are downsides to Facebook, and those downsides need to be considered before designing a branding strategy. A major downside is that Facebook is often lax in user protections. Not in terms of software or hardware security, those are generally safe. Rather, Facebook is not very good at ensuring users are courteous to each other. A user may be able to ban an abuser and erase his or her abusive posts, but Facebook rarely ban abusers. There are certainly situations in which Facebook bans or closes user accounts, but rarely is it due to things such as harassment. This means a company must plan ahead and ensure it has a competent public relations employee. Human nature is to get defensive when they are being attacked, but more often than not a company ends up looking worse when they attempt to fight back. There are certain companies that have managed, but by and large, the companies have to simply take the abuse and hope that blocking the user from their page will work.

In addition, Facebook isn't really designed for ease of use. This is because Facebook's main purpose is to get information on its users and sell that information to marketers and other companies. While Facebook wants and requires users to feel comfortable, by and large, people are forced to accept user-interface changes. A company may be able to maintain its Facebook page the way it wants, but if Facebook makes it difficult for a user to actually utilize the features or find the group, then it is not very useful. And Facebook does make it more difficult for users to find things. Interface changes such as reworking the way posts from followers show up (rather than simply allowing users to see posts in the order they were posted), changing up which posts they see and how often, and other counterintuitive changes often leave groups and pages high and dry as half of their followers suddenly stop seeing their posts. Because of this, Facebook can be difficult to manage. It is something of a double-edged sword, allowing a company to reach multitudes of potential customers. Yet at the same time, a company that relies on Facebook as its major marketing outlet can easily figure out what to do if half of its followers stop seeing its posts. Hard to market to people who don't know you exist. Even so, Facebook is nearly a requirement for any business that wants to be online.

Branding on Twitter

Twitter is a fascinating online service that mimics a blog, but has a maximum number of characters, requiring that users be as brief as possible with their words. Because posts are so short, a good PR (Public Relations) manager needed to run the company's Twitter account is essential. Excellent communication skills are essential for Twitter as every word has to count. Still, this "microblogging" site is as useful as a real blog in building an online brand identity, but it definitely requires a different skill set to make it work. The main advantage of Twitter is that it is fast and efficient for communicating simple ideas. Additionally, there is the complex but essential world of hashtags. Hashtags are additions to a post that begin with the "#" symbol followed by a keyword or phrase without any spaces between them. Though these count toward the users' limits on the size of their post, they will ensure that the microblogging posts (known on Twitter as tweets) appear in the searches and feeds of other Twitter users who are interested in the subject of these hashtags. Using hashtags is a fantastic way to build a brand, but one should be very careful which hashtags he or she uses.

Naturally, the most popular hashtags of the moment are advisable for building a brand. Unfortunately, with the chaotic state of the world, some of these hashtags are political in nature. While some companies may not mind being seen as taking a stance on political issues, others may well want to avoid the entire situation altogether to avoid alienating potential customers. That said, not every popular hashtag on Twitter involves a hot button controversy that could get a company's public relations department in trouble with its customer base. Of course, it is possible for a company to start its own hashtag, though this should be approached with caution. Hashtags for events can create an image of your brand in the mind of the public, without the cost of paying money to sponsor an event. A hashtag about a music festival will show up in the feeds of users searching for that music festival, associating a company with the style of music happening there. In a similar vein, sporting events, holiday events, comic book conventions, museum exhibitions, public festivals, and important days in history oftentimes have hashtags associated with them. Learning these hashtags, generally done by simply going to Twitter and spending time looking up hashtags, is a great way to associate a brand with nearly anything Twitter users are talking about.

The main downside of Twitter is that there is a lot of white noise in there that can be hard for a company to get noticed in. Millions of people use Twitter hourly while they are conscious and many established celebrities and companies tend to get the vast bulk of the attention. Even using all the most popular hashtags cannot ensure that a Twitter feed will be noticed, let alone followed. With so many users posting so many tweets, it is much like being in a massive room where everybody is talking and only a select few have access to a microphone that lets them actually be heard. This is quite a dilemma for anyone working toward e-branding, but there are some ways to help.

The best way to work toward getting attention on Twitter is to simply attach links to a brand's Twitter feed on other social media websites, as well as that brand's website. From there, a company Twitter feed should get at bare minimum a daily update on things that are important, whether it is a bit of written comedy related to the company's brand, an update on the latest release of a new product, commentary on a situation somewhere in the world in relation to your brand, or nearly anything else that can be condensed into less than 200 characters. In addition to providing advantages in SEO, a Twitter feed is an easy way to allow customers to connect with a brand in a high-tech way that takes almost no effort. That said, a social media manager handling a Twitter account for a brand must know how to write an amusing post with hardly any space to write it in. Each character counts, let alone each word, and a social media manager must make each of them have a maximum impact.

In a similar way, there is the depressing phenomenon of tweet wars where two or more Twitter users use their Twitter feeds to verbally attack other users in text. Twitter's administrators simply do not have the ability to stop every user recruiting violent radicals for extremist groups, let alone stopping the multitude of trolls and other abusive users. Getting into a tweet war is generally a very bad move, as it makes a company look unprofessional. Of course, there are PR managers who can successfully engage in a tweet war, but it is still a bad idea if done too often. And as is the way of human nature, many people think they are much better at such things than they really are. This is a mistake that can send a company into a tailspin if it is not careful.

Branding on Instagram and Tumblr

There are a few websites other than Twitter and Facebook that allow people to connect over the Internet. However, they are fairly specific and not a great fit for every company. The other two major ones are Instagram and Tumblr, each of which has a specific niche.

Instagram is a site designed for sharing images. People who follow an Instagram account will then have the option of leaving a message in a sidebar of the page the image is on. It is rarely a conversation, because it is not really set up to have that kind of interaction. Instead, the idea behind Instagram is that companies, celebrities, and everyday users can show off images showcasing either their brand or their everyday lives (which are also designed to showcase their brand if they're doing it right). This is a great tool if a company wants to have a more relaxed, casual voice to its brand. Allowing potential customers to see images of the company work site, the employees doing their job, and new and creative innovations is a great way to let them feel like they're part of the family. It creates a welcoming atmosphere and suggests that a company is willing to be transparent about itself and what it does.

The downside of Instagram is that it has the same problem as any uploaded image on the Internet. Once an image is uploaded to the web, it is there forever. Not only that, but these days photo manipulation is easier than ever. Programs like Photoshop allow people with almost no skill to crop and alter images. While it is unlikely that people will presume altered images from a company's work site are real, it creates a very real problem for any company dealing with the situation. If the company says something, it runs the risk of backlash in the form of people saying they should have a sense of humor. If it doesn't say anything, it is possible that people will begin associating the altered image with its brand more than its actual logo. Even worse it could be used in court in order to argue that the company is no longer protecting its trademark, because the company allowed that particular use of its trademark goes by without statement. Instagram is only as useful as long as a company is transparent and interesting. In order to judge if Instagram is a good tool for e-branding, the question of whether or not people want to see the pictures must be answered. If a marketing intern heads into the company building and finds plenty of interesting, uncontroversial things to take pictures of, then an Instagram account may work. If that intern has to stage pictures and disrupt work flow in order to get anything interesting, then it may be better to avoid Instagram altogether.

Tumblr has a myriad of problems that make it difficult to properly utilize for e-branding. Ostensibly a blogging site, Tumblr has changed its user interface so many times in so many different ways that it can often be difficult to find anything. The original idea of Tumblr was similar in nature to LiveJournal, in that it gave users their own space to upload longer posts and writing. However, Tumblr sharing isn't straight forward. Users have to follow a Tumblr feed, and while they can reply to a post the response isn't actually posted directly to the user to whom they're responding. Rather, original post is then uploaded to their own feed, with the addition of their comment. This often makes it difficult to follow conversations, though people often try. This can result in a pileup of conversations that never quite follow a logical flow. The end result is that people on Tumblr wind up following people rather than conversations. The outcome of this is that clever responses and user interactions happen in a much different way. Rather than attempting to archive posts, Tumblr users are encouraged to simply repost an entire conversation as it comes across their feed.

The practical effect of this is that Tumblr ends up working in much the same way as a brainstorming session done via e-mail. In fact, Tumblr conversations often end up looking exactly the same as e-mails that have been forwarded multiple times. This isn't to say Tumblr has no use in e-branding. In order to use Tumblr, a company has to be prepared to have no control over its messages on occasion. When something gets posted to Tumblr, users will reblog it at random. This makes it difficult to keep a coherent message, which makes branding difficult. However, if a brand's voice is relaxed and open to brainstorming, then Tumblr can work quite well.

Branding on Review Sites

There are an ever-growing number of websites dedicated to nothing more than allowing customers to leave reviews of a business. This grew from online auction and sales sites such as E-Bay and Amazon, which allowed buyers to leave reviews of sellers or products. Soon, websites began encouraging people to leave reviews of not just products or specific sellers, but restaurants, individual franchise locations, and specific stores.

These sites can offer amazing opportunities for small businesses wanting to break into the online market. Because these sites are specifically designed to help users find local businesses, it allows a company to ensure a certain amount of traffic to one of their physical locations. If the company is just a small start-up, that could be their only location. As such, ensuring they have a good reputation in the physical world can help them springboard into the online world as they offer current customers the ability to shop online and bring their products to new people across the globe. Of course, the problem with this is that these websites have little to no oversight in terms of fake reviews. Not that it would matter, because in most cases it is a "he said/she said" type of situation. With no oversight and the anonymity of the Internet, many people will choose to post extremely negative reviews. So, any company that wants to use review sites to help build its brand has to walk a careful line between not giving in to unreasonable customers and trying to keep their review scores positive.

Then there is the issue of buying reviews, both positive and negative. Much like with social media followers, there are companies who will buy reviews. They hire another company to write up reviews, both positive for their own company and sometimes negative ones for other companies and then attempt to reap the rewards. Unfortunately, this often works. Because these review sites have almost no oversight, there is no one to fix the problem. These sites generally allow companies to send in a claim, and the review might be removed. But then, it might not, and the company can do nothing about it. If a company wants to use a review site to build its brand, buying positive reviews is a fairly good idea. However, it is important not to overdo it. Too many good reviews, or reviews that seem overly positive, can often be a red flag that the review is bought instead of natural. If it becomes obvious the company has purchased reviews, it tends to lose quite a bit of business. No one wants to give their money to a company who lies to them, after all.

Buying Followers, Is It Worth It?

No matter what it is, if someone will buy it, then someone will sell it. This includes social media followers. The key to using social media for e-branding is having enough followers to make a difference. A company could have the best Facebook posts and post the most amazing messages on Twitter, but these do nothing if there is no one to see them. What is more, even if people see them they also have to share the posts. If more people aren't constantly following a social media account, then the account stagnates and becomes pointless. To that end, there are companies who will sell followers. For a specific price, which varies depending on the company and the exact services, an official social media account can gain thousands of followers in a short period of time. The benefits of this are obvious, and it would seem like a great idea. However, like all e-branding tools, it might not be a good idea for every company and every brand.

If a company is building a more stoic, professional brand then buying followers might work quite well. The fact that these followers generally have limited interaction with the company is not very important because the company is not trying to seem conversational. If a company is simply having straightforward, professional comments and responding only to the questions asked, then the fact that so few people respond simply does not seem that odd. However, many companies are trying to foster a more open, casual brand voice these days. Such a voice makes it much easier to become part of the community on any social media website. Being part of an Internet community is absolutely vital if a company is going to become a top brand, and only companies that are already top brands can generally afford to have a more sterile voice.

That said, it might be beneficial to buy a small number of followers, just enough to inflate numbers but not so many as to make it obvious when they do not respond. This course of action can be a good idea if a company is just starting out and hasn't entirely solidified a brand voice yet. With a small number of natural followers and a high enough follower count that potential customers won't think the company isn't worth the interest, a company can try a variety of different voices. It is much easier to throw things at the wall and see what sticks when there aren't many people to notice the mess. Ultimately, buying followers is beneficial in only a limited number of situations. It is generally more cost effective to hire someone who can devote all his or her work time to managing the various social media accounts and grow followers naturally. By the time a brand can benefit from buying followers, there is generally no need. Still, a company must decide for itself what is and isn't useful in overall marketing activities and brand building.

Summary

If a company wants to make it in today's world, it should possess an online brand. Yet not every tool is right for every company, as this book has shown. While a company can certainly find reasons to utilize every single tool that e-branding has to offer, most companies can get by with a Facebook and Twitter account and some targeted SEO work in order to get their company website noticed by Google. Generally, only the more niche companies need to worry about utilizing the more esoteric e-branding tools. Even so, the Internet is constantly changing, and things that were important fade into obscurity all the time. There are many websites that were once a cornerstone of Internet entertainment, only to have become forgotten and have their servers shut down. Sometimes, this is simply unavoidable. Markets change, people change, and some brands simply aren't a good fit for the world that comes after that change.

This is why e-branding is so vital for any business that wants to succeed. It may seem counterintuitive, given e-branding is all about making potential customers attracted to a company's brand rather than specifically the product or service. It makes sense when the breakneck speed of the Internet is taken into account. Twitter hashtags are always becoming popular and forgotten, with new ones to jump on to every single day. Video-sharing sites such as YouTube change their search algorithms, making all new videos go viral and top name YouTube personalities fade away. The practical effect is that keeping on top of e-branding allows a company to stay on top of what's most important to current culture. By knowing what social trends to connect with, and which social trends should be avoided at all costs, a company is able to subtly shift the appearance of its brand. This shifting allows a company to bring its brand, its voice, and its products and services to the modern world without becoming symbols of ages past.

And at the end of the day, that is what e-branding is all about. Ensuring a company is able to stay competitive and remain noticed without having to completely reinvent itself. Ensuring a company can stay part of the conversation on what customers want out of their industry. And allowing customers to feel as if they're not just clients but they are friends with the company. If history has proven anything, it is that people want to identify and associate themselves with brands that allow them to proclaim themselves a part of something. All a company has to do is figure out the trends and hang on for the ride, provided it is taking care of its brand.

Bibliography

Amaldoss, W., & Jain, S. (2015). Branding conspicuous goods: An analysis of the effects of social influence and competition. *Management Science*, *61*(9), 2064-2079.

Brems, C., Temmerman, M., Graham, T., & Broersma, M. (2017). Personal Branding on Twitter: How employed and freelance journalists stage themselves on social media. *Digital Journalism*, *5*(4), 443-459.

Faganel, A., & Janeš, A. (2015). Branding trends 2020. In *MIC 2015: Managing Sustainable Growth; Proceedings of the Joint International Conference, Portorož, Slovenia, 28–30 May 2015* (pp. 91-97). University of Primorska, Faculty of Management Koper.

Kedzior, R., Kedzior, R., Allen, D. E., Allen, D. E., Schroeder, J., & Schroeder, J. (2016). The selfie phenomenon–consumer identities in the social media marketplace. *European Journal of Marketing*, *50*(9/10), 1767-1772.

Kolb, B. (2017). *Tourism Marketing for Cities and Towns: Using Social Media and Branding to Attract Tourists*. New York: Routledge.

Machado, J. C., Azar, S. L., Carvalho, L. V. D., & Mendes, A. (2015). Motivations to interact with brands on Facebook–Towards a typology of consumer–brand interactions.

Manthiou, A., Rokka, J., Godey, B., & Tang, L. R. (2016). How social media marketing efforts influence brand equity creation and its consequences: The case of luxury brands. In *Let's Get Engaged! Crossing the Threshold of Marketing's Engagement Era* (pp. 561-561). New York: Springer International Publishing.

Nguyen, B., Yu, X., Melewar, T. C., & Chen, J. (2015). Brand innovation and social media: Knowledge acquisition from social media, market orientation, and the moderating role of social media strategic capability. *Industrial Marketing Management*, *51*, 11-25.

Severi, E., Ling, K. C., & Nasermoadeli, A. (2014). The impacts of electronic word of mouth on brand equity in the context of social media. *International Journal of Business and Management*, *9*(8), 84.

Shen, B., & Bissell, K. (2013). Social media, social me: A content analysis of beauty companies' use of facebook in marketing and branding. *Journal of Promotion Management*, *19*(5), 629-651.

Tenderich, B. (2014). *Transmedia Branding*. H. Schmidt, & J. Schmidt (Eds.). EIMO.

Thomas, S. L., Bestman, A., Pitt, H., Deans, E., Randle, M. J., Stoneham, M., & Daube, M. (2015). The marketing of wagering on social media: An analysis of promotional content on YouTube, Twitter and Facebook. North Melbourne: Victorian Responsible Gambling Foundation.

Tsimonis, G., & Dimitriadis, S. (2014). Brand strategies in social media. *Marketing Intelligence & Planning, 32*(3), 328-344.

Zavattaro, S. M. (2016). Some ideas for branding via social media. In S. M. Zavattaro, & T. A. Bryer (Eds.). *Social Media for Government: Theory and Practice* (p. 60). New York: Routledge.

CHAPTER 6

New Frontiers to a Digital Revolution

In this chapter, you will read:

1. New technologies that shape new frontiers
2. User-generated content
3. New users versus brands
4. The new habits of your digital brand

Introduction

Technology has changed the way firms and users communicate with each other. It is extremely clear by now that a higher level of personalization and app engagement is crucial. The key is not just thinking about the user experience in app, but the user experience being created around the app. Most of the mobile phone users spend their time on apps. It doesn't mean that they will use any type of apps. Users are becoming more and more selective regarding the usage of the apps. For that reason, the browsers still continue to drive more traffic.

It makes perfect sense then that firms are trying to follow that trend and all their efforts are concentrating on how they could deliver an awesome experience to their mobile targets. The problem is that mobile and web at some point converge. The key here is to be able to provide for both media the same experience. Don't overpromise on your website and underdeliver in your app. It's a very thin line in the converging app and mobile-web experience. In both cases, what you need to do is personalization. Personalization is the key to future success. A more personal and engaging app and website that will be focused on content and discoverability, rather than friction and discrete downloads, will lead you to success.

New Technologies That Shape New Frontiers

Technology is not everything! Of course, technology has helped us to change the way we communicate with our users but becoming digital is something more than that. Becoming digital should be more about a change in the mindset and the philosophy of our firm. Apparently, most firms can use digital media, because the required budget is relatively small, but not all firms are ready to change their mentality. By changing their mentality means that they need to find a new way to conduct their business and this is where the problem begins. If higher management doesn't have a common vision regarding how the company should become digital, then a lot of missed opportunities and bad performance will occur. As we discussed, the need of becoming more digital is initiated from the changed behavior of the users. It means that your firm needs to adjust the core values and enhance their delivery. That is after all the whole concept of becoming digital. You should be open to readjustments and, in some cases, you should be open to changing completely your business model. It all depends on the nature of your business. At the same time, you should keep in mind the constantly changing behavior of your users. Their expectations as well as their decision journey are constantly changing.

An extremely important aspect of becoming digital is to find out how you can improve your overall customer service. Right now, we are not talking about the user journey but also how your digital capabilities can design and deliver the best possible experience, across all parts of your business. Your mentality should be about implementing a cyclical dynamic where processes and capabilities are constantly evolving based on inputs from the customer, fostering ongoing product or service loyalty. Something like this is not easy to happen. All of your decisions should be based on relevant data that you have collected from your users. At the same time, all of your actions should be based on delivering content and experiences that are personalized and relevant to the users. You should make full use of analytics in order to understand your customers' real-time behavior, which is the one actually that will determine the type of communication you will have with them. If you don't feel comfortable using analytics, then you should outsource. That is the only way to understand the underlying behavior of your users. By doing so, you will be able to improve the customers' experience.

The new frontiers of the digital environment indicated extremely high levels of automation. This type of automation of course is not just an e-mail sent to the user. The automation should be extremely personalized as well as in real time. The users constantly interact with your firm, and in order for you to support this dynamic, you need to take it to the next level. We have already discussed in previous chapters the different types of automations you could make use of. It is certain that automation of customer interactions can boost the number of self-service options that help resolve problems quickly, personalize communications to be more relevant, and deliver consistent customer journeys no matter the channel, time, or device. Essentially that could mean, having lower running costs and higher probability to understand customer needs and wants. Overall, a digital mindset institutionalizes cross-functional collaboration, flattens hierarchies, and builds environments to encourage the generation of new ideas. Incentives and metrics are developed to support such decision-making agility.

Apart from just changing their mentality, firms have in their hands new types of technologies. More and more brands are experimenting with virtual reality as well as with interconnectivity, in the sense that connected devices could help building stronger and more meaningful relationships with the users. Virtual reality is a great opportunity to understand customers and have a live feedback of their most inner thoughts and behaviors. It is one thing for someone to be able to hold a branded experience in their hands on a mobile phone, and another to feel as if they are inside a branded experience on their virtual reality headsets. We should not take light that this type of close relationship has raised some concerns from the user's side. Users are getting tired of any type of interruptive advertising; so imagine if your firm is more intrusive than that. In order to be successful, publishers, advertisers, and technology companies will need to come together to develop creative ad formats that truly put the user first, in order to create new standards and benefit from the new "mobile only" world order. Undoubtedly, virtual reality is adding a totally new perspective in e-branding. A new perspective is far more equitable than any other previous technologies. The great thing about this new type of technology is that it changes the way we communicate. Virtual reality is giving a new way to meet a brand's objective and redefine the way that customers engage and revisit your products or services in the long term.

Apart from virtual reality, another type of technology that reshapes the frontiers of digital branding is wearable tech. More and more firms are launching new accessories that either work as stand-alone products or need to be connected to the smartphone of the consumer. Although wearable items used to be quite expensive breakthrough products, now we are witnessing a lot of low priced products in the sector. Especially in the fitness sector, wearables have gained the broadest acceptance among consumers. The question that firms are facing now is if the consumers will continue to buy limited-function devices when their smartphones can deliver a lot of the same value. For example, smart watches are often designed as smartphone extenders, allowing users to see messages and caller ID without taking out their phones and are the category where fashionistas are making their mark.

User-Generated Content

User-generated content is the next big thing in e-branding. Most of the millennials are being influenced more from the user-generated content, than from any other form of advertising. That is so simple and it makes so much sense, yet it's very difficult to be applied from most firms out there. One thing is for sure that there is a huge shift away from ads and product promotion, and closer to personalization and visualization in content marketing and social media. The only thing that needs to happen is for marketers to activate not only their customers but also their employees as well as their partners to start creating content.

It has been quite difficult in the past years for somebody to create high-quality content. With the use of today's affordable technology and with the plethora of free software programs, anybody could create high-quality content. To make it even easier, the only thing an average consumer will need in order to do so is a smartphone and some free apps! More and more users are creating content every day. More and more apps are being designed around that very concept. Users must create the content in order to appeal other users. Apps like InstaStories, SnapChat, and Facebook Live are just some examples of user-generated content. Consumers are getting more and more comfortable with shooting and sharing their content. At the same time, firms have started to realize the immediate impact of user-generated content in their sales.

The reason why user-generated content is more appealing to the new generation is just because it emits an inherent authenticity. Users who watch the content could somehow connect with it because they get a feeling of familiarity. They could also be the ones, in any given stage, who will upload similar content. Because we have already established the power of user-generated content, it's time that we have a plan to capitalize on this new trend. How can we use this type of content? One thing we could do is to collect all the videos from our followers and edit them into one branded video. Sometimes, of course, that might be extremely difficult to do so. What you can do is just ask initially your employees to collect videos that they have created. Don't forget that your employees are your ambassadors, given that you treat them as your customers. You should encourage them to use their phones and shoot videos in company's events or even during normal working hours in terms of giving some behind-the-scenes footage. You could even create an internal contest on the company's Facebook page and give some incentives to the web page fans with prizes.

Crowdsourcing video is one of the greatest ideas in terms of gathering user-generated content, and even if you don't have the capacity to create a video, it is very cheap to outsource it. If you want, you can use some extremely easy apps to do it yourself. If you play your hand right, you can gather some amazing content. But as we discussed, users will not just do it by themselves. They need a nudge and this is where your input is important. If you manage to create a video, from the material given by your users, you could have something intrinsically shareable and perfect for social media. At the same time, you minimize your costs, because you wouldn't need any professional team. If the video that was taken from the users seems unprofessional, it just makes it more believable. That is the brilliancy behind it. All users know that they can't create any extremely professional video and it makes perfect sense for them if they watch something a bit unprofessional. It reassures them that the content is coming from the users and not from the company.

New Users versus Brands

Globally, users are making their smartphones part of their everyday routine. This is a truth that everybody acknowledges. The key though is to be able to capture consumers in crucial everyday moments where buying decisions are bound to happen. Those moments are the ones you should be focusing on. The new type of user is called Social Local Mobile (SoLoMo). Social networking sites like Facebook, Twitter, and Instagram are growing rapidly as channels of human communication, allowing brands and consumers to engage in public discussions. As consumers are using social media as their main source of information, communication, and entertainment, marketers will be finding a fruitful environment full of opportunities. The rapid proliferation of advanced smartphone and other mobile devices allowed people to exchange information by pinpointing consumers' location and providing them on their mobile devices with location-specific advertisements. The integration of mobile advertising with location-based services is what characterizes location-based advertising. Smartphone penetration has increased for two reasons. First, wireless networks have become faster and ubiquitous. Second, mobile devices are nowadays more affordable. Mobile marketing can provide consumers with personalized information based on their location and the time of receipt. Having in mind this new type of users, we need to focus on how we can reach them through digital branding. For this reason, we first need to check their search intent, which are basically more crucial than their actual demographics. This is based on the simple motion that when users are ready to shop, what they want matters much more than who they are.

A very interesting new trend on e-branding is YouTube. The importance of online video has been recognized by the marketers. They all understand it but it's incredibly difficult to harness it. Just the idea of managing another media platform creates a new heading. But what you need to realize is that this online platform could create a total new dimension for your brand. You should not overlook the fact that a lot of people still watch a lot of television. Hence, this traditional type of media remains an extremely useful tool for a marketer. If you are already spending some marketing budget on TV advertising, then you should think of spending 10 to 20 percent, depending on market maturity, of that budget to YouTube, which is a people-focused neutral platform. You will not have to create new ads but you could use the same add with some tweaks or if you have the extra budget, you could develop new advertising campaigns.

Because you will spend fewer budgets and at the same time you will be able to have a more targeted campaign, you could lengthen your campaign and improve the coverage. By doing that, you will be able to create a top-of-mind awareness for your brand, which is one of the key purchase drivers across a wide range of industries. The clear media implication is a need to be on air all year round, but this is often challenging given campaign-led approaches and the sizes of media budgets. That is why online video is the new and extremely powerful tool, but at the same time a controllable opportunity, to just add some messages in between your media campaigns. You shouldn't worry if you don't have a big budget in order to create new campaigns. There are a lot of companies that you could outsource by investing a small amount of money. You could use some super-user partnerships, which make it possible to create additional content in a flexible and affordable way. I must stress here the fact that serious marketers should be looking to drive meaningful paid scale behind every execution. What you need to realize is that in order for your campaign to be effective, you should be consistent. At the same time, you can't just drive true media continuity just by posting content and hoping people find it.

The marketing budget is getting lower and lower each year and that is why you need to think twice before allocating your communication expenditures. Just a low budget online video initiative can drive meaningful reach and business results. You don't have to spend lots of money as long as you target correctly. Many firms out there underestimate the amount they should spend on online video, and as a result only tap into a fraction of the audience. For a big brand that spends millions on TV, it's time that YouTube's budgets were six figures, not just five. When you include the impact of skipped views, then you start to see the huge potential scale that is currently ignored. One of the main differences between TV and online advertisements is that, by definition, the TV ads are limited to a specific location and often at one specific time of the day, depending on the audience you want to target. On the other hand, online video ads (mobile or laptop) don't suffer those limitations. That is the many reason why they are becoming more and more popular. At the same time, people are watching more and more online videos because it's more convenient for them to do it while on the go. Next time you are in the train, try to notice that most people who are on their phones are watching some sort of clips. Most of the times, they are directed to those clips through a social media platform. Almost without trying, brands will find that something like a third of their paid YouTube activity already lands on mobile, but the opportunity to specifically target and optimize for it is only just being explored. There are, of course, some key creative watch-outs, in particular, that sound is often muted or that attention spans are even shorter on smaller screens. We have analyzed over the previous chapters the different types of strategies that you could employ in order to build a strong online brand with the use of social media. Increasingly, this also includes the opportunity to reach new consumers in developing markets for the very first time, though data access can be a challenge here. One of the main problems with the online video is that this type of new user has been used on over exposure to online ads. You need to be able to cap the frequency of adverts for users in order to prevent overexposure.

One of the ways to succeed this arduous task would be to personalize the ads. It is a huge field that few brands have explored. The opportunity to reach people with subtly or radically different creatives based on who they are and what they are doing should be the next frontier in digital. Imagine if you could provide slightly different types of ads in order to target different groups of people. The effectiveness of your communication campaign would hit the roof. Another great benefit of this type of targeting is that it would allow you to tell sequential stories to the same consumer. That would just take it to the next level of branding. You would be able to build a strong narrative over time or even actively push them along a purchase funnel. Of course, another huge benefit of online video, when it supports the new brand, is the ability to click on it. Video advertising is hugely powerful when passively consumed but when it's online, there is also an option to click immediately and explore or even buy something. When establishing a new brand in the electronic environment, online video is the most powerful tool that you could use.

The new type of consumer is ready to replace the TV ads with the online ones. For most brands, online video won't begin to truly replace TV until there's a much more substantial shift in consumer media consumption. At the same time, there are a few brands that already maximize the huge opportunity that is already there. And don't forget the future. Viewing habits are beginning to radically change and marketers would do well to understand how their marketing can too.

New Habits of Your Digital Brand

We are living in a time where technologies are converging. This is creating a social and economic revolution that's transforming the way we live and work. It's transforming not only what we consume, but how we consume. There are a few new trends that could transform your brand. These new trends should be the new habits of your digital brand. All of these trends and new habits represent a new opportunity for brands and marketers to engage with people in new ways.

The power of the crowd is getting more and more attention. It doesn't really matter for what use we decide to involve our users, as long as they believe that they are a part of our brand. Of course, it is very difficult to harness the network power of many individuals. We could use individual users for crowdsourcing. Many big firms have already put this idea into motion. Crowdsourcing is basically involving your users to participate in the creation of your new products or services. Imagine how your users would react if one of their ideas was actually implemented by your firm. They would feel that they have the power to create new products or services. In fact, in order for you to discover what they would like, you would have to perform market research and that would cost you money and time. Now, with crowdsourcing, you could do it a lot cheaper. So, basically you need to think the ways through which you can bring ideas from the outside in. Along with crowdsourcing many firms now employ crowdfunding. Crowdfunding is nothing more than pooling lots of donations from individuals.

Another new habit of your digital brand is something that we discussed in a previous chapter and that is the SoLoMo user. This trend involves using digital tools to create face-to-face, real-world interactions. It's the combination of social (trust), local, and mobile. This type of user should be the center of your attention. You can do that by employing social design. Social design basically puts your users, and not your product or content, in the center of the overall experience. It involves building online communities instead of marketplaces by allowing the social network to become a "trust network."

What firms need to realize is that the electronic environment is changing rapidly. A few years ago, people wanted to buy products or services online. There was an emerging trend whereby consumers want to buy things online. Of course, many consumers still want to do that. But a new trend is emerging. Users no longer want to own products or services. Instead, their focus is on the needs and experiences these products fulfill. This is seen in the shift from an asset-heavy lifestyle to the asset-light generation. For example, the physical ownership of music, movies, and books has shifted to on-demand access. As the meaning of ownership is being transformed, we need to ask ourselves how it will transform what we value and how should we express our brand.

Bibliography

Brabham, D. C. (2008). Crowdsourcing as a model for problem solving: An introduction and cases. *Convergence, 14*(1), 75-90.

Brands, S. A. (2000). *Rethinking Public Key Infrastructures and Digital Certificates: Building in Privacy.* Cambridge: MIT Press.

Burdea G., & Coiffet, P. (1994). *Virtual Reality Technology.* London: Wiley-Interscience.

Carpenter, P. (2000). *eBrands: Building an Internet Business at Breakneck Speed.* Boston: Harvard Business School Press.

Cha, M., Kwak, H., Rodriguez, P., Ahn, Y. Y., & Moon, S. (2007, October). I tube, you tube, everybody tubes: Analyzing the world's largest user generated content video system. In *Proceedings of the 7th ACM SIGCOMM conference on Internet measurement* (pp. 1-14). ACM.

Daugherty, T., Eastin, M. S., & Bright, L. (2008). Exploring consumer motivations for creating user-generated content. *Journal of Interactive Advertising, 8*(2), 16-25.

Estellés-Arolas, E., & González-Ladrón-De-Guevara, F. (2012). Towards an integrated crowdsourcing definition. *Journal of Information Science, 38*(2), 189-200.

Krumm, J., Davies, N., & Narayanaswami, C. (2008). User-generated content. *IEEE Pervasive Computing, 7*(4), 10-11.

Kuppuswamy, V., & Bayus, B. L. (2015). Crowdfunding creative ideas: The dynamics of project backers in Kickstarter. *SSRN Electronic Journal.*

Mollick, E. (2014). The dynamics of crowdfunding: An exploratory study. *Journal of business venturing, 29*(1), 1-16.

Rheingold, H. (1991). *Virtual Reality: Exploring the Brave New Technologies.* New York: Simon & Schuster Adult Publishing Group.

Ryan, M. L. (2001). *Narrative as Virtual Reality: Immersion and Interactivity in Literature and Electronic Media.* Baltimore: Johns Hopkins University Press.

Yan, J., Liu, N., Wang, G., Zhang, W., Jiang, Y., & Chen, Z. (2009, April). How much can behavioral targeting help online advertising? In *Proceedings of the 18th international conference on World wide web* (pp. 261-270). ACM.

Breuer, R., & Brettel, M. (2017). Time lags and synergies of online advertising. In Campbell, C. L. (Ed.). *The Customer is NOT Always Right? Marketing Orientationsin a Dynamic Business World* (pp. 917-917). Cham: Springer.

Vizhi, T. K., & Sridhar, P. (2016). A study on advertising in social networking sites and its implications on consumer buying behaviour. *PARIPEX-Indian Journal of Research, 5*(8).

Index

OTHER TITLES IN DIGITAL AND SOCIAL MEDIA MARKETING AND ADVERTISING COLLECTION

Victoria L. Crittenden, Babson College, *Editor*

- *Corporate Branding in Facebook Fan Pages: Ideas for Improving Your Brand Value* by Eliane Pereira Zamith Brito, Maria Carolina Zanette, Benjamin Rosenthal, Carla Caires Abdalla, and Mateus Ferreira
- *Presentation Skills: Educate, Inspire and Engage Your Audience* by Michael Weiss
- *The Connected Consumer* by Dinesh Kumar
- *Mobile Commerce: How It Contrasts, Challenges and Enhances Electronic Commerce* by Esther Swilley
- *Email Marketing in a Digital World: The Basics and Beyond* by Richard C. Hanna, Scott D. Swain and Jason Smith
- *R U #SoLoMo Ready?: Consumers and Brands in the Digital Era* by Stavros Papakonstantinidis, Athanasios Poulis and Prokopis Theodoridis
- *Social Media Marketing: Strategies in Utilizing Consumer-Generated Content* by Emi E. Moriuchi
- *Fostering Brand Community Through Social Media* by William F. Humphrey, Jr., Debra A. Laverie and Shannon B. Rinaldo
- *#Share: How to Mobilize Social Word of Mouth (sWOM)* by Natalie T. Wood and Caroline K. Muñoz
- *The Seven Principles of Digital Business Strategy* by Niall McKeown

Announcing the Business Expert Press Digital Library

Concise e-books business students need for classroom and research

This book can also be purchased in an e-book collection by your library as

- *a one-time purchase,*
- *that is owned forever,*
- *allows for simultaneous readers,*
- *has no restrictions on printing, and*
- *can be downloaded as PDFs from within the library community.*

Our digital library collections are a great solution to beat the rising cost of textbooks. E-books can be loaded into their course management systems or onto students' e-book readers. The **Business Expert Press** digital libraries are very affordable, with no obligation to buy in future years. For more information, please visit **www.businessexpertpress.com/librarians**. To set up a trial in the United States, please email **sales@businessexpertpress.com**.

www.ingramcontent.com/pod-product-compliance
Lightning Source LLC
Chambersburg PA
CBHW071149200326
41519CB00018B/5167